Tak ... ls to Israel

A Guide to Family Fun in the Holy Land

Updated 2019 edition

Aileen Kirschenbaum

Ben Yehuda Press
Teaneck, New Jersey

Published by Ben Yehuda Press
122 Ayers Court #1B
Teaneck, NJ 07666
http://www.BenYehudaPress.com
ISBN13 978-1-934730-77-5

19 20 21 / 6 5 4 3 2   20190616

Take Your Kids to Israel

Aileen Kirschenbaum

Dedication

This second edition of *Take Your Kids to Israel* is dedicated to our daughter Shani's memory, and in her merit we hope to share our love and joy for Israel with you.

Shani's love of Israel and sense of adventure inspired all who knew her. Shani was born on Yom Haatzmaut and grew up in Plainview, New York. She attended the Hebrew Academy of Nassau County through high school where she passionately advocated for the State of Israel. She worked for ZOA in Washington and interned with Congressman Steve Israel on Long Island.

Shani attended Stern College of Yeshiva University. She went on to study nursing at Columbia. She worked at St. Francis Hospital and then continued her studies to become a Nurse Anesthetist. She excelled in her chosen profession, winning a national competition among nurse anesthetists.

Together we roamed Israel far and wide, enjoying everything from its people and workshops to eateries and watering holes. She loved art, animals, hiking, swimming and skiing. Her love for Israel was boundless, though she held a special place in her heart for Netanya. Her happiest moments were spent in Israel with family and friends.

Several projects have been undertaken in her memory: an award for Israel advocacy at Hebrew Academy of Nassau County; a scholarship fund to support a student nurse through the Achoteinu program LINK; an Israel tour program in the girls' Yeshiva of Sderot; and donations to Wounded Soldiers in Israel.

A special thank you to my family for all your patience and input. I appreciate you trying out many of the sites for me. Josh, Shanee, Rami and Oren, Michael and Jenny, Rebecca, Adam and Leah, I couldn't have done it without you. Rebecca, thanks for your *editing*. To my husband Ben, thanks for the countless hours spent traveling, researching and working out all the glitches. I love you guys.

Shoshana Yaffa z'll

Courtesy of Carta

Table of Contents

Introduction

This book is meant to be a guide for English-speaking families who want to tour Israel with their children and grandchildren. Whether this is your first trip, or you *live* in Israel, there is something for everyone. Some places are appropriate for teens and others for young children. I have tried to give a brief explanation of each place to help you decide if a particular place is appropriate for your family.

Our family has been touring Israel for thirty years and we are always finding new and exciting places to visit. Try to rediscover Israel through the eyes of your children. Ride a camel, climb a mountain, wade through a stream.

Our philosophy when traveling with children is to create a positive experience for children of all ages so that they would want to return at the earliest opportunity. They should develop a love and deep connection to the land and people of Israel. Details of history will come at their desired pace.

Included are many suggestions for children of all ages. I must *emphasize* to **call ahead** wherever you go. Hours of operation change with the day and the season. Often places have extended hours during holidays and in the summer. Other places are closed during holidays. In the winter, sites close early. Please call ahead and make reservations whenever possible.

I have included as many phone numbers and web sites as possible; but once again, they are subject to change. It's always best to plan ahead.

Best Time to Visit

You can visit Israel year-round. There is no bad time to visit Israel. From May through September there is no rain at all, so every day can be an outdoor day. July and August are *very* hot, so it is best to mix in some water activities daily. The holidays are beautiful in Israel, but many Israelis are on vacation so there are larger crowds at many of the sites, and you need to reserve places further in advance. The weather from November until March is variable, but mild compared to the northeastern United States.

Travel Tips

Waze and Google Maps work very well in Israel. Inputting destinations in Hebrew works best, but English also works. You may need to try different variations in spelling.

Always carry water. Conventional wisdom is don't leave your car without water!

If you are planning a long visit (two weeks or more), you may want to consider renting an apartment. You generally get a lot more space and it's more economical. You won't get breakfast or maid service, but you can eat out for many meals for the amount you save over staying at a hotel.

National Parks

National parks are generally open from 9:00 A.M. to 5:00 P.M. April through September, and from 9:00 A.M. to 4:00 P.M. October through March. However, hiking trails often will not admit groups anywhere from two to four hours before closing time, as they want to make sure you are out before dark.

If you plan to visit more than six national parks, buy a discount card called a Green Pass. They are available for purchase at the major parks. There are several different options depending on your length of stay, number of parks you wish to visit and whether you plan to return within the year.

If you are visiting during Sukkot or Pesach, the national parks often run special events. Look for the events in newspapers and online.

Website for all national parks: www.parks.org.il

More Information

Museums: Museum hours are very variable. Some open as early as 8:00 A.M., and others open at 10:00 A.M. Closing hours also vary. Some museums are only open half a day; others close late. Fridays are always different from other days of the week. Hours also change with the season. Check the museum website or call for hours.

Electricity: The electrical current is 220-volt AC. 110 appliances can only be used with a step-up transformer and appropriate adapter.

VAT: This is value added tax. There is an 18% tax on most goods and services in Israel. At most retail stores it is included in the price. If you make a purchase of $100 or more and are taking the product out of the country, you can have your V.A.T. tax refunded. You should fill out a special form at the store. You present this form along with your purchases at the airport for a refund prior to your departure. Tourist services such as hotels and hotel meals are exempt from V.A.T.

Cellular Telephones: Multiple options exist. You can rent phones before you go, or at Ben Gurion Airport. Perhaps the easiest option is to purchase a SIM card and a plan for the amount of time you'll be going. It is illegal in Israel to drive while holding cell phones. Many rental cars are equipped with Bluetooth, so ask your rental agent about this.

Newspapers: You can get the baseball scores and other news from two English newspapers in Israel: The Jerusalem Post and Haaretz. On Friday the Post also has Shabbat times listed for the major cities.

Minyan: If you are looking for an Orthodox minyan in Jerusalem any time of the day or night (at least until midnight), you will find one in Katamon in the Shtiblach on Hachish Street.
godaven.com/detail.asp?Id=284

Important Phone Numbers

Police: 100
Ambulance: 101 Magen David Adom
Fire: 102
Information: 144
Israel Country Code: 972

US Embassy:
14 David Flusser
Jerusalem 9378322, Israel
Phone: 02-630-4000
Tel Aviv Branch:
Rehov Hayarkon 71, Tel Aviv
03-519-7475

US Consulate: 02-622-7230

Canadian Embassy:
Rehov Nirim 3/5, Tel Aviv
03-636-3300

Tel Aviv: Taxi Nordau Tel. 03-546-6222
Netanya & Herzliya: Taxi Hashachar Tel. 09-882-2222
Jerusalem: Taxi Rechavia Tel. 02-622-2444
            Bar Ilan-Navi Tel. 586-6666, 581-4444

Tipping: Most people tip 10% in a restaurant. A tip of 15% or more is considered very generous. Israelis generally do not tip taxi drivers, so any amount is appreciated.

Where to Stay
With Jerusalem or Tel Aviv as a base, many places are accessible for day trips. The Upper Galil and Golan are one exception. A recommendation for accommodations in the north is Kfar Giladi. It is a child-friendly kibbutz with a large indoor pool and moderate breakfast. It is close to many of the attractions in the north. Ask for the more recently renovated rooms.

Beaches

This small country has an amazing number of beautiful beaches. Cities along the Mediterranean coastline offer licensed beaches with lifeguards, showers, changing rooms, and cafés. All the major cities, like Nahariya, Akko, Haifa, Netanya, Herzliya and Tel Aviv have public beaches. The Dead Sea attracts people from all over the world and features hotels with spas and beach access. The Red Sea at Eilat offers beaches, water sports, reefs, and dolphin encounters. The Kinneret is Israel's only freshwater lake. The beaches here range from rocky to soft sand. Currents can be tricky. Please swim where there is lifeguard supervision.

Always Use Sunscreen

It is important to remember that the sun in this region is stronger than in Europe and most of North America. Bring lots of sunscreen and use caution.

Always observe the flags on the beach. A white flag means waters are calm; a red flag means to swim with caution and a black flag often means swimming is forbidden.

Geography Lesson

We always posted a map of Israel on the refrigerator and circled the places we visited. It was a great way to learn the geography of Israel.

The most important thing is to *plan, plan, plan* and then enjoy. You will create memories that will last a lifetime!

Details in this book were accurate at press time; however, changes often occur. If your experiences are different from those listed please let me know: Takeyourkidstoisrael@gmail.com

The Talmud says, *"One who walks a distance of four cubits (six feet) in the land of Israel is assured of being an heir to the World to Come.* (Ketubot 111a) Imagine how much spiritual merit your family can gain in all your miles of sightseeing and adventuring!

Useful Websites:

For up-to-date information and new sites: www.takeyourkidstoisrael.com

Egged Buses: www.egged.co.il

Israel Railroad: www.rail.co.il

National Parks: www.parks.org.il

Restaurants and discount coupons: www.eluna.com

Special services for disabled tourists who visit Israel
www.friendsofyadsarah.org

For celebrations
(Bar/Bat Mitzvahs, weddings and chesed/mitzvah projects):
www.celebrateisrael.com/

www.emunah.org/bar-bat-mitzvah/
or call 212-564-9045

Brothers For Life Experience:

Soldiers allow families and groups the opportunity to experience Israel through the eyes of an IDF fighter. They will plan activities for you. Options are ATV, jeeps, simulation training, and extreme sports. Good for Bat and Bar Mitzvah experiences.

www.brothersforlife.com   03-5622789
                                                       03-5598242

For an evening activity, almost every city in the country has an *Escape the Room* adventure game.

www.escaperoom.co.il/en

Jerusalem

Kiryat Yovel: Monster Slide. Imagine what this looks like through the eyes of a child!

Monster Slide (Mifletzet): Not far from Har Herzl is the monster slide. It is a very large sculpture with three red tongues that serve as slides. Give kids a chance to unwind at this amazing looking slide and famous landmark of this community.

Rabinowitz Garden   Kiryat Yovel

Herzl Museum and Mount Herzl: Located here is the memorial gravesite of Theodore Herzl, the father of Zionism, along with many famous Israeli citizens, among them Golda Meir and Yitzchak Rabin. The Herzl Museum is a state-of-the-art interactive museum with audiovisual effects and recreations of meetings and events in Herzl's life. The tour takes about one hour. This is like a visit to Epcot. Reservations are a must. This visit reconfirms your pride in Israel.

Har Herzl	02-632-1515
Mount Herzl, Jerusalem	www.herzl.org.il

Yad Vashem: This is a true memorial to the Holocaust. It includes a new synagogue, artifacts from destroyed European synagogues, an audiovisual center, and an archive of films related to the Holocaust. Among its many unique exhibitions is the Avenue of the Righteous Among Nations, Valley of the Communities, and the Children's Memorial. Also on display is a cattle car in which Jews were shipped to extermination camps. This is truly the Jewish people's memorial to the 6 million who died in the Holocaust. Ages 10 and up.

Yad Vashem	02-644-3400
Jerusalem	www.yadvashem.org

Givat Ram

Israel Museum

Israel Museum and Shrine of the Book: The Dead Sea Scrolls are housed in a white domelike structure in this museum. The shape of the pavilion is similar to the lids of the jars in which the Dead Sea Scrolls were found. Next to the shrine is the Billy Rose Sculpture Garden. In the main building you will find the interior of a 18th century synagogue brought here intact from northern Italy, a 19th century reconstructed German synagogue, and a wooden 16th century synagogue from India. There is also a youth wing where hands-on exhibits and workshops may interest children.

Givat Ram	02-670-8811, 02-670-8873
11 Rupin Blvd.	www.imj.org.il

The Knesset: Observe the Knesset in session or take a guided tour. Only open a few days a week. Reservations and passports a must!

Ha Kirya	02-675-3337
	www.knesset.gov.il/

Jerusalem Bird Observatory: Israel lies at the heart of one of the world's busiest migration routes. Many birds stop here to refuel. The observatory offers a variety of activities for families, including making birdhouses. Walk through the paths of migrating birds or sit in a shelter and watch the birds in their natural habitat. Good for children of all ages. A night safari is also available.

Adjacent to the Knesset,	52-386-9488, 02-653-7374
at the end of Rothchild Street	www.Birds.org.il

Supreme Court Building: The court is open to the public. Children of all ages are welcome. You can sit in on a court session or take a tour. English tours are at noon.

Givat Ram	www.gov.il
Sha'arei Hamishpot Street	elyon1.court.gov.il/eng/home/
02-675-9612/9613	index.html

Jerusalem Botanical Gardens: This is a gem in the heart of Jerusalem. It contains a large and diverse collection of plants from around the world. They offer independent and guided tours for all ages. Ask at the desk for a Young Scientist's Backpack with activities and a magnifying glass! There is also a Children's Discovery Trail to learn about how plants grow. They often have special programs and exhibits.

1 Zalman Shne'ur Street (Entrance on Herzog Street)	
02-679-4012	www.botanic.co.il

Bloomfield Science Museum

Bloomfield Science Museum: Exhibits change and evolve constantly in this museum. People of all ages and backgrounds will enjoy the interesting and interactive exhibits and activities. There are also demonstrations and do-it-yourself workshops. Recommended for both kids and parents. Parking is free but it fills up quickly. There is also paid street parking.

Near Hebrew University at Givat Ram

Museum Boulevard   02-654-4888

www.mada.org.il

Bible Lands Museum

Bible Lands Museum: This museum focuses on the history of the biblical era. It shows the different cultures of the people mentioned in the Bible. Check for special family events.

Givat Ram   02-561-1066
Museum row   www.blmj.org
21 Shmuel Stephan Weiz Street

Downtown Jerusalem

Gush Katif Museum: This museum tells the story of the Jewish settlements in the Gaza strip from the days of the Hasmoneans until the uprooting of the Jews in 2005. The story of the struggle is outlined by artifacts, photographs and videos. The museum is only two rooms, but it is packed with information. Hours are short. Call for opening times. Best for teens and up.

    5 Shaarei Tzedek Street   en.gushkatifmuseum.com/
    02-625-5456

The House of Rabbi Kook: The house of Rabbi Avraham Yitzchak Kook gives good insight into the rabbi. The former beit midrash has a film about his life. Guided tours are only available to groups.

    9 Ha Rav Kook   02-623-2560

Museum of Underground Prisoners: This museum reconstructs the struggle of Israel's underground members: Hagana, Etzel and Lehi leading up to the establishment of the State of Israel. This used to be a British jail. More appropriate for older children.

    Russian Compound   02-623-3166
    1 Mishol Hagevura Street

Museum of Italian Jewish Art: This Italian Synagogue was transported to this museum from Conegliano, Italy after World War II. It contains a collection of items from the earliest centuries and depicts the life of Jews in Italy.

    25 Hillel Street   02-624-1610
                             www.ijamuseum.org

Friends of Zion Museum: FOZ is an interactive, experiential museum. It tells the story of our non- Jewish friends over the last two centuries, whose efforts helped establish the state of Israel. You are accompanied by a tour guide. The tour lasts one hour. Reservations are recommended. The recommended age is 7 and up.

    20 Yosef Rivlin St.   02 532-9402
                             www.fozmuseum.com

Hebrew Music Museum

Hebrew Music Museum: The museum has on display collections of original ancient instruments. An iPad accompanies you on the tour. You scan the number next to the instrument you would like to find out about and it gives explanations and information about the instrument. You are also able to hear the sound of the instrument. The tour includes multimedia musical games, movies and a virtual reality experience. You can spend an hour or more here. The décor in each room is beautiful. You can ask for a guided tour or a special guide for children who will teach them about rhythm and allow them to try some of the instruments. Truly a great addition to the museums of Jerusalem!

10 Yoel Salomon Street   02-540-6505

www.hebrewmusicmuseum.com

Ben Yehuda Street: This is Jerusalem's open-air pedestrian mall. Sit and have a bite to eat at any of the outdoor cafés and shop the stores and vendors.

Yad Eliezer Volunteering: Yad Eliezer provides nourishment to needy families as well as empowering them to achieve self-sufficiency. Volunteers visit the warehouse and assist in packing food. This is a hands-on opportunity to learn about giving to others. Parking at the warehouse is free. To volunteer at the Jerusalem warehouse, email: volunteers@yadeliezer.org

Romena, Jerusalem   www.yadeliezer.org.il

12 Shimshon Polanski Street

Time Elevator: This attraction is a Disney-style ride through Jerusalem's history. The audience is seat-belted and given headphones for the journey that begins at the time of King David and Solomon and ends with the Six-Day War in 1967. The story includes the birth of Christianity and the emergence of Islam. The simulator ride concludes with an aerial ride over the Jerusalem of today. This ride is for kids 5 and up and lasts about 25 minutes. There are stationary seats for those who prefer them. Time Elevator is closed on Shabbat.

Agron House   02-624-8381

37 Hillel Street   www.time-elevator-jerusalem.co.il

Mea Shearim: This neighborhood was founded in 1874. It was one of the first urban communities outside the Old City walls. Its residents have preserved the traditional ways of Jewish life that existed in northern and eastern Europe. When you explore Mea Shearim you should dress modestly. Women should wear dresses with long sleeves. Men need long pants and a hat. The main marketplace is located through the iron gate on Ein Yaaqov Street. You can purchase all types of Judaica items here such as kipot, shofars, mezuzah cases, challah covers and silver. There is also fresh produce.

Machane Yehuda

Machane Yehudah: Many native Jerusalemites do their weekly shopping at this shuk, filled with fruits, nuts, vegetables, baked goods and all types of souvenir shops. It is a very busy market, especially before Shabbat, and worth the unique experience.

Jaffa Road, west of King George

Bite Card Tour at Machane Yehuda: Explore Machane Yehuda with a self-guided audio tour on your smart phone. Pick up your Bite Card along with a map for 105 NIS. Bring earphones to learn more about the shuk as you make your way around. The bite card has several choices, both meat and dairy to choose from. You can wander the shuk and try new foods as well as some favorites. Some of the portions are large enough to be a full meal. You probably can't use the card up in one visit. This is by far the best way to experience the shuk. Highly recommended!

en.machne.co.il/

Kol HaOt workshop

Kol HaOt: Explore Jewish texts, history and values through interactive workshops, special exhibits and events. Experience hands-on workshops that explore a Jewish text or topic. Every member of the group will come home with a memorable creation from their experience. First, tourists are introduced to a variety of artworks. Then, participants design their own project that illuminates a traditional Jewish text or concept. Truly a wonderful opportunity for families with a wide range of ages!

Kol HaOt   050-790-4964

www.kolhaot.com

The Bloc: Rock Climbing for all ages. Children under 16 must have a parent with them.

7 Yitzchak Elishar   02-539-8991
                                             www.thebloc.co.il

JClay Pottery Studio: Create your own Judaica themed pottery. Paint a washing cup, mezuzah, dish and so much more. No age limit and no experience necessary. You can make a reservation or walk in. You will have to return a few days later for pickup. There is a small fee per painter of 20 NIS and then fees starting at 25 NIS for the item of your choice.

Mekor Baruch-Shuk   02-678-6828
14 Yosef ben Matityahu Street   www.jclaystudio.com

House of Levi Eshkol: This is the house of the former Prime Minister of Israel from 1963-1969. The tour features an excellent video (with English subtitles) of the contribution of a key founding father of the state of Israel. The house has furniture from the time period as well as many pictures of previous prime ministers who also lived in the house. A walk down memory lane. Good for teens interested in history.

46 Ben Maimon Street   02-625-2357, 02-631-3091
Rehavia   www.levi-eshkol.org.il

Teddy Kollek Park: This beautiful park was named for the Mayor of Jerusalem from 1965-1995. The water fountains run every hour and kids can have fun running through them. Adults can enjoy the sound and light show in the evenings. There is no shade, so bring caps and drinks. Daytime shows at 10:00am, 12:00, 4:00 and 6:00. Evening shows: 8:00, 9:00 and 10:00pm. Entrance to the park is free; there is paid parking on the street on in the Carta Parking lot.

Pele Yoets, Mamilla   02-675-1711
www.tod.org.il/en/museum/teddy-park/

Hutzot Hayotzer: This artist colony allows you to explore the art galleries here, meet the artists and hear their stories. It is one of Jerusalem's oldest and most beautiful cobblestone streets. Artists can often be seen working in their studios. Also located here is the Teddy Kollek visitors center. This is a small museum dedicated to this famous mayor of Jerusalem.

Hutzot Hayotzer, Artist's Colony   artistscolony.co.il/home-page

Old City

Cardo, Jewish Quarter

The Cardo: In the 6th century, the Cardo was Jerusalem's main street. Today, as in the Roman days, the Cardo is a shopping mall with many exclusive galleries and shops. Below the Cardo are remains of the ancient shops and stalls.

www.rova-yehudi.org.il/sites/the-cardo/

Jaffa Gate: As you enter Jaffa Gate, there is a tourist information center on your left. This is a good time to pick up maps and information. Next to the office between two trees you can find the tombs of the men said to be architects of Suleiman's city walls. The walls were built between 1536 and 1542 by the Ottoman sultan Suleiman the Magnificent.

Kotel (Western Wall)

Western Wall: (The Kotel): The Kotel, the Western Wall, is the holiest and most significant Jewish site in the world It is the remains of the outer wall of the Second Temple courtyard. Jews have returned here for centuries to mourn the destruction of the Temple. You should dress modestly for your visit. It is a place for prayer; people often write notes and prayers and place them in the crevices of the ancient stones in the wall. This site is always open.

Jewish Quarter, Old City of Jerusalem   02-627-1333

www.thekotel.org

Western Wall Tunnels: The Western Wall is only the beginning of an amazing trip through history. Register for a tour of the tunnels, a continuation of the outside wall. It begins with a historical account of the area and a model for you to see where you are. You will proceed to walk deep into history through some spaces both vast and narrow, built more than 2,000 years ago. The tour includes virtual models. It is one of the must-see sites in Jerusalem.

Jewish Quarter, Old City of Jerusalem

Tower of David/Museum of the History of Jerusalem: This museum tells the history of Jerusalem over 5,000 years, until 1948, and is located at the Tower of David, a citadel built by King Herod near the Jaffa Gate. This museum is not filled with artifacts, but uses models, holograms and videos to explain the city's history.

Tower of David, Jerusalem   02-626-5333
www.tod.org.il/en/museum/about-the-museum/

Tower of David/ Night Spectacular: If you are in Jerusalem, do not miss this. The walls of the citadel serve as a stage for a nighttime sound and light show that tells the story of Jerusalem. It lasts about 45 minutes. This show is enjoyable for everyone! It may be cool even in the summer, so bring a sweater.

David's Citadel   www.tod.org.il/en/
02-626-5333   the-king-david-show/

Virtual Reality Stories and Games from the Bible: This virtual reality activity is fun and educational. Climb out of Joseph's pit, get rid of the snakes, answer trivia questions, and take a roller coaster ride through the land of our patriarchs. Recommended for ages 6 and up, as you need to be able to read. Takes about an hour.

072-3940564   www.tbe.org.il

The Jewish Quarter through mosaics: These nine stunning mosaics are on display in the Western Cardo, where the ancient marketplace once was. Worth a visit!

Wohl Archeology Museum: An excavated complex with a 385-foot section of the Upper City and several ritual baths. You can buy combination ticket for the Wohl Museum and the Burnt House.

Jewish Quarter, Old City of Jerusalem, 1 Hakara'im Street

02-626-5906   www.ilmuseums.com

www.rova-yehudi.org.il/sites/the-herodian-quarter/

Temple Mount (Har Habayit)

The Temple Mount (Har Habayit): Inspiring and fascinating, a visit to the Temple Mount will change your perspective. The size of the Temple is hard to imagine without walking its entire length. We strongly recommend taking a guided tour as guides know how to make this a smooth process. You might want to stop first at the Davidson Center to learn about the structures on the Temple Mount, so you can correlate what is there now with what was there before the destruction by the Romans. The footprint of the Temple is clear and easy to navigate with a guide.

Southern Wall

Southern Wall Excavations: You can visit on your own, but a guide is highly recommended. The remains here are so vivid you can picture yourself buying your sacrifice for the Temple. The marketplace still has walls from the stalls, the ends of the arch are still visible, as well as the crushed walkway, which remains from the destruction of the Temple. Highly recommended.

    Old City   02-626-5906

The Davidson Center: This center is located in the Jerusalem Archaeological Park. The site offers the history of the Temple Mount. The center consists of several galleries containing recently excavated objects from the Second Temple period, the Byzantine period and the Umayyad period.

One of the main attractions here is a virtual reality reconstruction of the Herodian Temple Mount prior to its destruction. Also see a high definition video describing Jewish pilgrimage to Jerusalem during the Second Temple period. Reserve in advance.

Jerusalem Archaeological Park   02-626-5906
www.rova-yehudi.org.il/sites/archaeological-park-davidson-center/

Ramparts Walk: Enter the ramparts at Jaffa Gate for a whole different perspective of the Old City. From here you can really see how people live inside the city, especially the Muslim Quarter. The walk from Jaffa Gate ends at Lions' Gate. It is not possible to make a complete circle on the ramparts. You will be most comfortable if you go in a small group.

Jaffa Gate, Old City of Jerusalem

A Look into the Past: Virtual Reality Tour of the Temple: This attraction is located on the men's side of the Western Wall Plaza. Participants receive headphones and virtual reality glasses. Sit in a swivel chair and take a 10-minute journey back 2,000 years to the Temple. Hear the **Levi'im** sing, and walk around the Holy Temple. Reservations are not required. Purchase tickets where you purchase the tunnel tour tickets. Great for the whole family.

Western Wall   02-627-1333
                                          www.thekotel.org

Burnt House: During the Second Temple period, this was the basement workshop of the Bar Katros family. Here, more than anywhere else, is evidence of the fiery destruction of the city by the Romans. See the audiovisual presentation to put the artifacts in context.

Jewish Quarter, 2 Hakaraim Street   02-626-5906
www.rova-yehudi.org.il/sites/the-burnt-house/

Temple Institute: At this institute you can view actual sacred Temple vessels produced by the institute, according to the exact Biblical requirements. They are being prepared for use in a future Holy Temple. They also have original oil paintings, which recreate the story of daily life in the Temple. There is a 25-minute audiovisual presentation, and private guides are available.

Old City   02-626-4545
40 Misgav Ladach Street   www.templeinstitute.org
Look for signs saying "Treasures of the Temple"

Hurva Synagogue

Hurva Synagogue: If you haven't been to Israel in several years, you will remember this synagogue as just an arch marking the site where an 1864 synagogue had been destroyed by the Jordanian army in 1947. In 2010, the synagogue was rebuilt and rededicated. You will hear the history of the synagogue and see the beautiful murals on the walls. See the aron kodesh and walk around the outside terrace for some incredible views. Reservations are necessary.

02-626-5900   www.rova-yehudi.org.il

Siloan Pool and Tunnel

City of David: An archeological site believed to be the original capital of King David. A 3,000-year-old, 6-foot wall has been found; it is believed to have belonged to David's palace. Pottery was also found from the time of David and Solomon, along with official seals from the times of the prophet Jeremiah. This site includes the Gihon Spring, Siloan Pool and a 400-meter tunnel that is nearly 4,000 years old. These were all parts of water systems that supplied the city throughout the ages. This is the most exciting part of the tour; but be aware that it is about a 40-minute walk through water that often comes up to the hips of an adult. It is dark and very narrow in most places. You must go single file and carry a flashlight. There is no turning back once you get started. There is now a dry tunnel that is much shorter and larger than the water tunnel. It includes a short movie inside. For anyone who does not want to go through the water this is a great alternative.

Shiloach Village, City of David Visitors' Center

02-626-8700   www.cityofdavid.org.il

02-626-2341   bit.ly/tyk2david

City of David Sound and Light Show

City of David Sound and Light Show: The City of David presents a unique sound and light show that tells the story of the rebirth of Jerusalem. It is set on the ruins of the city of David under the night sky. I highly recommend this show for all ages; however, there are many steps to climb. A free shuttle departs from the first station parking lot and is available to take you back to the first station as well.

City of David National Park   077-996-6726
                                                www.cityofdavid.org.il

Zedekiah Cave, Solomon's quarries: An enormous cave, five city blocks long, under the Muslim quarter of Jerusalem. The stones for the buildings of ancient Jerusalem were quarried for King Solomon here.

East Jerusalem, near the Damascus gate
02-627-7550

Temple Mount Sifting Operation: In 1999, the Muslim wakf began construction on the southeast side of the Temple Mount, a site known as Solomon's Stables. Vast amounts of land were removed from the Temple Mount. The Temple Mount Antiquities Salvage Operation is currently engaged in sifting through the tons of land and other material from the site. The findings continue to astound visitors with discoveries of artifacts dating back to the First and Second Temple periods. Become an archaeologist for the day and help sift through the dirt at stations set up for the task. Allow about 1½ hours.

Operated by the City of David Emek Zurim National Park
35 Shmuel ben Adaya Street
Parking at Beit Orot car park-Mormon University
Walk down the footpath from the parking lot (About a 5-minute walk)
02-626-8724, 077-996-6726   www.cityofdavid.org.il

Israel Scaventures: Navigate your way through streets, alleys or markets, while learning about the neighborhood. You will receive maps and mission packs to begin your scavenger hunt. Great family and group activity. Hunts take place in the Old City, Nachlaot and the shuk. There are also Scavenger hunts in Tel Aviv and Tzfat.

052-835-8072   www.Israelscaventures.com

Northeast Jerusalem

Ammunition Hill

Ammunition Hill: (Givat Hatacht Moshet) During the Six-Day War this was the scene of a decisive and costly battle. The trenches have been preserved, creating an open memorial to the soldiers who reunified Jerusalem. Kids will love playing in the trenches.

   5 Zalmon Shragai Street   02-582-9393
                                            www.g-h.org.il

Southeast Jerusalem

Segway tour on the Haas Promenade

Segway tours: This is run by Ir David. Ride a Segway and get an overview of the ancient city of Jerusalem. This is a guided tour on the Haas Promenade. You should be 16 years old to drive a Segway, but sometimes they are a bit more lenient. The tour takes about 1½-2 hours. Great for teens! This promenade is also a wonderful place to see a panoramic view of the Old City. There is a park here for children to play.

Haas Promenade   02-561-8056

www.segway-jerusalem.co.il

Hasmonean Aqueduct Tour: Over 2,000 years ago, two aqueducts were built to bring water from the Pools of Solomon to the Temple in Jerusalem. Explore the remnants of the lower aqueduct and learn about their historical significance. The tunnels no longer contain water; they are dry! This is not a tour for claustrophobic people. Baby carriers are not permitted, and you will need a flashlight, which you can purchase on site.

Armon Hanatziv Promenade at Statue of the Birds

02-626-8700   www.cityofdavid.org.il

02-626-8724

Southwest Jerusalem

Ein Lavan

Ein Lavan: Just past the aquarium is a short walk to two beautiful springs. One is shallow enough for young children and the second one is deep enough for swimming. There are beautiful views at the top as well. There are about 50 steps to the springs. Strollers may be difficult to manage.

Jerusalem Mall (Malcha Mall): This mall is one of the largest in the Middle East. It includes a supermarket, department store, several movie theaters and almost 200 restaurants and shops, including *Pizza Hut.* This is not in the food court, which has a very large selection of eateries as well.

    Derech Agudat Sport Beitar 1   Off Begin Boulevard

Rock Climbing Wall: This is a rock-climbing facility on the eastern side of Teddy Stadium. It is for beginners and advanced climbers. Hours are mostly late afternoon and evening.

    Malha   02-648-2264

Gottesman Family Israel Aquarium

Gottesman Family Israel Aquarium: Recently opened is the new aquarium in Jerusalem, next to the Biblical Zoo. Its main purpose is to educate the public on the challenges facing Israel's aquatic ecosystems: the Mediterranean Sea, the Red Sea, the Dead Sea and fresh-water habitats. This is truly a state of the art facility. It includes an underwater viewing tunnel and diving presentations. Note: Tickets for the aquarium do not include admission to the zoo next door.

Derech Aharon Shulov   972 73-339-9000

Gazelle Valley: A lovely park and now a nature preserve is home to several gazelles, wading pools, walking paths and biking promenades. The site is handicap accessible. If you are going for the gazelles you are better off at the zoo, as they are usually quite a distance away from the paths. That being said it is a lovely place for a long stroll. The park is free.

Opposite the Pat Intersection at the Begin Highway
02-992-7699
www.itraveljerusalem.com/ent/gazelle-valley/

The Tisch Family Zoological Gardens: (Biblical Zoo) Over 1,000 mammals, birds, reptiles and amphibians live in this zoo. Many paths are wheelchair and stroller accessible. There is also a zoo train, which gives you access to some of the upper level exhibits. You must purchase a ticket at the Noah's Ark Visitors Center to ride the train. The visitor center features interactive computer stations and a gift shop. The surroundings are beautiful and there is a nice petting zoo. Note: Tickets for the zoo do not include admission to the aquarium next door.

1 Derech Aharon Shulov   02-675-0111
                                   www.jerusalemzoo.org.il

Ein Yael: This is an outdoor, hands-on children's museum. It recreates ancient art and craft techniques in Jerusalem. You can make pita, pottery, paper from scratch and much more.

Opposite the Biblical zoo, near the   02-645-1866
    Malcha Mall   www.einyael.co.il

Pantry Packers: Pantry Packers is part of Tikun Olam Tourism, packaging food for families living below the poverty line. Each visitor receives an apron, hat and gloves and is given a different station to operate. Stations include: sifting, bagging, labeling and packing. It's a great opportunity to have some fun and give back. Wear closed-toe shoes. Free parking.

1 Moshe Baram   02-626-0035
Talpiot, Jerusalem   www.pantrypackers.org

German Colony

German Colony: Templars from Germany arrived here during the 19th century, but the British exiled their pro-Nazi descendants during World War II. The neighborhood today has an Old World charm and its main street (Emek Refaim) is filled with cafés, restaurants and upscale shops which include jewelry and Judaica. On Fridays there is a craft fair/flea market at the Adam School at 22 Emek Refaim.

German Colony   02-545-8113
12 Emek Refaim   kadvchomer@ginothair.org.il

Team Karting: This is a go karting experience. Drivers must wear helmets and closed shoes. Children 8 and up can drive.

Lev Talpiot Mall, lower level   077-50-30-566
17 Haoman Street   teamkarting.co.il

First Train Station

First Train Station: Originally opened in 1892, this pedestrian mall was the first train station in Jerusalem. It has recently been completely renovated to resemble the train station, but is now filled with restaurants, shops and vendor stands. There is always a variety of entertainment and activities taking place here. There is a carousel, as well as a train which takes you around the pedestrian mall. There is also an indoor activity center for young children. There is something here for families of all ages. You can also walk or bike ride along the new tracks for miles, through a lovely park. Bike rentals are available.

4 David Remez   02-653-5239

www.firststation.co.il

Bowling: There are 18 American style bowling lanes, with bumper bowling available. There is also an arcade with prizes. The lanes are all computerized, so all you have to do is bowl!

Lev Talpiot Mall   02-678-2000

Kapon Defense Workshop and Shooting Range: Learn to defend yourself. Make a reservation for Krav Maga, Weapons Training, or Tactical Paintball. Activities are run by professional experts and take place in a state-of-the-art training facility.

13 Yad Harutzim, Talpiot   972-54-332-0777

www.kapondefense.com

Kad V'Homer: Paint your own pottery in this shop. There are over 100 items to choose from, including menorahs for Chanukah, washing cups, mezuzot, and honey pots. The customers are not only children! Prices range from 25 NIS to 200 NIS. Allow 5 days to pick up projects.

12 Emek Refaim   02-545-8113
German Colony

Begin Center: This is no ordinary museum! In a presentation lasting a little over an hour, experience the life and times of Menachem Begin, Israel's 6th prime minister. This multimedia program gives you modern history in an interesting way, along with the opportunity to see Begin's living room and sit in his chair. With this experience, you will feel very much a part of history.

6 Nahon Street (across from the Cinematheque)
02-5652020   www.begincenter.org.il

Cable Car Museum: During the War of Independence, Uriel Jefetz designed a cable car to link Mt. Zion with the Israeli position at St. John's Hospital in the western section of Jerusalem. The cable spanned 200 meters and was used only at night so as not to be detected by the enemy. The cable car was used for about half a year to evacuate the wounded, and deliver ammunition and supplies. Today, you can see the original cable car inside the hospital, now turned museum, as well as a beautiful view of Mt. Zion. Book this in advance. The museum is often locked.

Contact East Jerusalem Development, Ltd.
17 Hebron Road   02-627-7550
www.pami.co.il

Liberty Bell Park (Gan Ha Paamon): Across from Yemin Moshe, and next to the Inbal Hotel, you will find Liberty Bell Park. The park has beautiful paths for strollers with plenty of shade. It has great climbing facilities for children 12 and under, including a very large dinosaur. This park often hosts festivals and performances. Puppet shows go on all year.

Intersection of Keren Hayesod and King David St.
02-673-5029

Windmill at Yemin Moshe

Yemin Moshe: This is an affluent neighborhood with stone houses and well-kept cobblestone streets. The neighborhood was named for Sir Moses Montefiore, a prominent philanthropist who spent much of his life aiding Jews in distress. There is a windmill here, which will capture the interest of children. Montefiore had it built in 1857 for this area. It never actually functioned as a mill because there wasn't enough wind in the area.

Sderot Blumfield

West Jerusalem

Chagall Windows, Hadassah Medical Center: Marc Chagall created 12 windows and gave them to the synagogue when the hospital was new in 1959. Today Hadassah Hospital is one of the largest in the Middle East. You can see the windows by taking a tour of the Abbell Synagogue which includes a short film about the hospital.

Hadassah Medical Center   02-650-0670

www.hadassah-med.com

Tree Planting Experience: Participate in this tradition of planting a tree in a forest in Israel.

Keren Kayemeth LeIsrael-JNF   02-658-3349

www.kkl.org.il

Sataf: Sataf is located in the Jerusalem Hills and is famous for its hiking trails and natural beauty. There are a total of 5 hiking trails and springs. It is free to enter.

Sataf Junction   02-642-8462

Challenge Tours: Challenge tours offers rappelling and ropes courses in Jerusalem to families with children of all ages.

02-625-5738, 052-893-8921   www.challengetours.org

Around Jerusalem

En Hemed National Park

En Hemed National Park: This is a gem just outside of Jerusalem. It has many streams, small pools, and amazing Crusader ruins that children will love to navigate. It never really feels crowded as there is ample space and there are picnic tables for everyone. A great place to spend a few hours.

En Hemed   02-534-2741

Yvel Jewelry Factory: The Yvel Jewelry Factory is a great place to learn about jewelry making with pearls and precious stones. The tour lasts about 1½ hours. You will see a video about jewelry making and then walk past the artists as they work. At the end you can roam the factory store.

Motza   02-673-5811
                                                         www.yvel.com

Yad La'Shiryon

Yad La'Shiryon/Latrun: This is the museum and memorial site of the Armored Corps Museum. There is a movie (check for English) and an outdoor exhibit of over 200 tanks that were used in the region. Good for all ages.

1 km south of Route 1 on Route 3   08-630-7400/1
                                        www.yadlashiryon.com
                                        bit.ly/tyk2enhemed

Kif Tzuba

Kif Tzuba: This is an indoor/outdoor amusement park for toddlers and school age children. There are inflatable castles, a train, bumper cars, a large indoor play area and more. The roller coaster is great for young children. Get there early as they limit the number of visitors. Prices are greatly reduced the last few hours the park is open.

Kibbutz Tzuba, off the Jerusalem-Tel Aviv Road

02-534-7952   www.kiftzuba.co.il/

Galita Chocolate Workshop

Galita Chocolate Workshop: The chocolate factory up north has opened a chocolate workshop at Kibbutz Tzuba. This is a great activity for adults and children. The tour begins with a short video of the origins of chocolate and then you move to a special room for the workshop. Each person can choose the items they want to make. The chocolate is kosher and chalav Yisrael . Call for a reservation. Families can get a combined ticket for the amusement park and chocolate workshop.

Kibbutz Tzuba, off the Jerusalem-Tel Aviv Road
02-534-7000
www.tzuba.co.il, www.galita.co.il/en/order_workshop

Mini Israel Park: A delightful mini version of most of the prominent sites in Israel. This attraction features over 350 exact replica models of Israel's most important sites. Buses, cars, trams and cable cars move. It is quite extensive. Try to visit in the cooler parts of the day. Enjoy a 3D aerial movie of Israeli sites as well.

I km south of Route. I, in Latrun   1-700-559-559

Herodian National Park

Herodian National Park: This is in the Judean desert in the West Bank. The fortress built by King Herod was a summer palace with gardens and pools. This fortress is very well preserved and has revealed buildings from various eras, including pillared halls and bathhouses, store-rooms and water reservoirs. According to Josephus, the king was eventually buried here. Many archaeologists believe that they have found the burial site of King Herod at this fortress.

Call Efrat Visitors Center   www.minisrael.co.il
02-595-3591   bit.ly/tyk2herodium

Stalactite Cave Nature Reserve: (Soreq Cave): A stalactite cave that includes spectacular formations of stalactites and stalagmites. A lovely 150-step path takes you down to the entrance. There is a short film to watch and the guided tours are worthwhile. This tour is available all year round. No strollers are permitted in the cave. English tours are available upon request.
Avshalom Reserve, Near Beit Shemesh, Route 3866
02-991-1117   bit.ly/tyk2soreq

The Castel: This was the battleground for the struggle over the route to Jerusalem. Keeping this road open was essential to the Jerusalemites. Climb up this hill and see what the battle for the Jerusalem-Tel Aviv road must have been like during the War of Independence. A great place to play hide and seek.
Mevasseret Zion exit on the Jerusalem-Tel Aviv Highway
02-534-2741   bit.ly/tyk2castel

Kfar Etzion Heritage Center: Discover the history of Gush Etzion at Kibbutz Kfar Etzion. Visit the museum and see a dramatic movie portraying the beginning of the Gush Etzion Bloc, which was strategic in protecting Jerusalem from attack by the Jordanian Legion. Learn about the fall of The Gush Etzion settlements during the War of Independence in 1948, and its resettlement after 1967. Lasts about an hour. Reservations are recommended. For ages 8 and up.
02-993-5160   www.etziontour.org.il

Biyar Aqueduct: King Herod transported water to Jerusalem through this underground tunnel. It is wet and can be muddy. There are two pathways upon entering the tunnel. The path straight ahead requires some crawling. The walking path is to the right once you enter the cave. Each path takes about 20 minutes. It can be crowded during holidays. The walk through the water is only available in the summer and in warm weather. However, viewing the tunnel is possible all year round. Private tour a must. Parking is at the jug handle south of Elazar.
02-9935133   http://bit.ly/tyk2biyar

Pat BaMelach Bakery

Pat BaMelach Bakery: Enjoy a Biblical bread-baking workshop with David in his artisan bakery. Each workshop is tailored to fit your group's needs. David will provide you with the dough and instructions. While the bread is baking, you will hear a short presentation, also tailored for your group, on bread and the Tanach. Allow about 2 hours. Truly a one-of-a-kind experience!

Rosh Tzurim, Gush Etzion   02-502-0262

www.patbamelach.com

Teva Naot Factory Outlet: The outlet at Kfar Etzion offers a nice selection of Naot shoes as well as good prices.

Maof, Gush Etzion   02-993-8198

Gush Workshop

Gush Workshop: This is a true woodworking activity. Use real machinery and create your own unique Judaica product. Each person can choose a project and spend most of the time working on their creation. Everyone goes home with a beautiful work of art! You can also work on a project as a family. There are 2- and 3-hour sessions, priced accordingly. Recommended for ages 6 and up. Adults enjoy this as much as the kids.

Rosh Tzurim   www.etziontour.org.il
054-678-5813/   theworkshopgushetzion@gmail.com

Deer-Land: For those who like adventure this is a great place to visit. Deer-land has the longest zip line in Israel, and the second-longest in the world. If you prefer both feet on the ground, there are ATVs, jeeps, archery and paintball. There is an interesting ropes course, a small zoo and a petting area. Also available is a climbing wall, bungee jumping and rappelling. Open every day in the summer from 9:30-5:30, but it is best to call ahead. For ages 3 and up.

  Gush Etzion, Road #60 from Jerusalem or #367 from Beit Shemesh (Opposite
    entry to Kfar Etzion there is a small side road near the traffic circle)
  02-570-9768   deerlandal@gmail.com
             www.deer-land.co.il

Gush Etzion Winery: Take a tour of this award-winning winery. Tasting is included (adults only). There is also a café at the winery.

  Gush Etzion Junction   02-930-9220
             www.gushetzion-winery.co.il

Caliber 3: Caliber 3 is an anti-terror training site in the mountains of Gush Etzion. Families, groups or individuals can take a two-hour action-packed training session with professionals. Learn to shoot an M16 and a handgun. View an anti-terror demonstration and learn about protecting Israeli families from terror. This activity is suitable for ages 4 and up. Children under 17 will shoot paintball guns and anyone over 17 shoots firearms. This is an amazing experience but can be costly.

  Gush Etzion   02-673-4334, 050-342-2770
             www.caliber3range.com

Zomet Experience: Find out how rabbis and engineers solve technical/halachic problems together. Walk through an interactive exhibit and watch English or Hebrew movies. Take a guided tour or a self-guided tour. For ages 6 and up. Free parking.

  Alon Shvut, Gush Etzion   02-993-2111
  3 HaErez Street   www.visitzomet.com

Hebron

Hebron: Full-day guided tours are available to see the Jewish sights in Hebron. The main attraction is the Cave of the Patriarchs (Mearat Ha Machpelah) where Abraham, Isaac and Jacob, Sarah, Rebecca and Leah are buried. Tours will also take you to Rachel's Tomb in Bethlehem.

One such tour is: 052-431-7055

Hebron Fund Tour (full-day tour)   www.hebronfund.org

Rachel's Tomb: Rachel's Tomb is a site that has been sacred to Jews for many generations. It is a special place for prayer. There is no entry fee and it is open every day except for Shabbat. There is a parking lot at the tomb compound. Check security restrictions before you go.

Directions: South on Jerusalem's Hebron Road until you enter Bethlehem. At the roundabout turn right and arrive at a border police checkpoint. Follow the road until you arrive at the tomb.

GPS coordinates: 31N 43'09"x 35 E 12'07"

www.rachelstomb.org

Beit Shemesh Area

Biblical Museum of Natural History

Biblical Museum of Natural History: This museum put together by the "Zoo Rabbi," Rabbi Natan Slifkin, showcases many exhibits including live animals. It is part zoo, part natural history museum and part Torah education center. It includes an introductory movie about Biblical animals and then a 2-hour interactive guided tour including interaction with some of the animals.

Industrial Zone, Beit Shemesh   073-213-1662
5 HaTzaba Street   www.tevatanachi.org

Archaeological Seminars

Dig for a Day Archaeological Seminars: This is an archaeological dig for the whole family. Families enter a series of caves, once the basements of families of 2,000 years ago. Get shovels and buckets and begin digging in one of the cool, comfortable caves. With every dig you are sure to find pottery remains, bones and sometimes more complete treasures. After digging for about an hour, a guide will take you to explore some other caves already dug out. Children usually love this experience and come home with lots of souvenirs.

Beit Guvrin Road to Beit Shemesh   02-586-2011

www.archesem.com

Buster's Beverage Company: Busters offers a 30-minute tour of their family brewery. This is primarily for adult children, as they only make alcoholic beverages such as cider and beer. Younger children are permitted on the tour. If you choose to stay for a tasting there is a nominal fee and they will offer something non-alcoholic to the kids. You can add a beer workshop to your tour. Reserve in advance.

Nacham Industrial Area   054 638-1106
Sorek Industries Park #9   www.busters.co.il

Bet Guvrin-Tel Maresha National Park: The antiquities and archaeological site above ground are worth a visit, but the complex series of underground caves is the reason to visit this site. One complex is called the Columbarium, a huge underground chamber where it is believed pigeons were stored, probably for ritual sacrifices, though they could have been used as carriers or for food as well. Just off the road, on the opposite side of the tel, (in a parking lot) is another fascinating complex of caves. These were personal water cisterns and storerooms. Kids generally like exploring these chambers.

Beit Shemesh-Kryat Gat Road (35)   08-681-2957, 08-681-1020
Opposite Bet Guvrin Kibbutz   bit.ly/tyk2guvrin

Bell Caves (part of Bet Guvrin National Park): These caves were once a quarry from which the people extracted lime for cement. They date back to the second century and were probably not built to be inhabited, though at times it is believed people took refuge in them.

Beit Guvrin, Route 35   08-681-1020
                                          bit.ly/tyk2guvrin

Sofer Tour: Take a behind the scenes tour and learn about how Torah scrolls, mezzuzot and tefillin are created. Get a chance to write on parchment yourself. You can add calligraphy or paper-cutting workshops as well. The tour lasts about 2 hours and is good for ages 5 and up.

8/3 Nachal Katlav   02-999-1391
Ramat Beit Shemesh   www.moshebraun.com

Kakadu

Kakadu: Kakadu produces many of the beautifully painted wooden products you see in gift shops around the country. You can reserve a workshop here with the artist and make your own art project. This is a great activity for all ages if you enjoy painting. The artist will teach you and guide you to a lovely finished product. Activities are customized to meet your needs. Good for large and small groups.

29 Moshav Zafririm   052-862-5271, 02-999-8922
                                       www.kakadu.co.il

Speedi Kef: The real attraction here is the alpine slide cut into the mountain. Slide down a metal slide in a mini car. Kids will want to go several times. Adults can ride with very young children. There are bumper boats and a trampoline as well.

Mevo Betar, near Beit Shemesh   02-533-0260, 052-338-5029
                                       www.spee-di-kef.co.il

Adulam Nature Reserve

Adulam Nature Reserve: Off Route 38 opposite Kakadu is this beautiful nature reserve. If you follow the trail it takes about an hour, depending on how long you spend in the various caves.

02-996-9213   bit.ly/tyk2adulam

En Prat Nature Reserve

En Prat Reserve and Stream: Inhabited since the second century BCE, the reserve has a beautiful, 30-minute trail along the stream, which also includes a deep pool for swimming (if you don't mind the fish). The pool was built by the British to hold the water of the spring that emerged here. This is great for children. There are remains of settlements and monasteries along the trail, one of which is still in use. The reserve has more difficult trails as well. There are plenty of picnic tables, so bring lunch! Only 30 minutes from Jerusalem. More information and a map are available at the entrance.

To reserve climbing activities or guided tours call 02-570-9580
02-571-5859   bit.ly/tyk2enprat

Ma'aleh Adumim Area

Monastery, artist studio near Ma'aleh Adumim

Ma'aleh Adumim: This is an area where some people may find it helpful to have someone assist them in planning and driving around the area. I would recommend tour director Shelley Brinn. She can personalize family tours as well as large group tours of the area. There are many possible activities to enjoy, as well as some amazing sights to see. There is a children's program at the Moshe Castel Museum of Art, which includes a scavenger hunt. She also offers a family nature walk. For older children she offers a desert experience. You can also visit local artists in their workshops.

Tour Adumim   054-527-5404

www.touradumim.com

Good Samaritan Museum

Museum of the Good Samaritan: This is the only mosaic museum in the country and one of three in the world. Ancient mosaics and other artifacts unearthed in Israel are on display. Includes mosaics from ancient synagogues. Some of the mosaics have been removed from various sites to protect them, and others are reconstructions. There is a very enjoyable short movie about the Good Samaritan story from the Christian New Testament shown inside a cave. Mosaic workshops are available with a reservation.

Located on the south side of the main highway from Jerusalem to the Dead Sea

054-527-5404   www.touradumim.com

The Moshe Castel Museum of Art: The exhibitions at this museum feature the works of artist Moshe Castel (1909-1991). The artist's motifs are taken from the world of Jewish tradition, Bible, Kabbalah and the landscapes of Israel. The museum hosts lectures, events and workshops. Special workshops for children can be arranged through Shelly Brinn.

Kikar Hamuseum, Ma'ale Adumim   02-535-7000

www.castelmuseum.co.il

Tekhelet Factory

Tekhelet Factory: a nonprofit organization with individuals who devote their time to obtaining the snails that produce the blue dye used in ancient times for making tzitzit. The factory is located in Ma'ale Adumim. Request an English guide and you will be fascinated with the workshop and story behind the *tekhelet*. You can purchase a tallit or just one blue string for your own tallit.

Ma'ale Adumim   Toll-Free 1-877-446-0656

02-590-0577   www.tekhelet.com

Eretz Bereshit

Genesis Land (Eretz Bereshit): Experience life as it was in Biblical times, in the heart of the Judean desert, on the way to the Dead Sea. Visitors are greeted by Eliezer, Abraham's servant, and by camels which take you to Abraham's tent. Once you are in the tent you can taste the fruits of the times, create mosaics, bake pita, reconstruct pottery, mold clay, and more. This is a wonderful program for children and young teens.

Yishuv Alon   02-997-4477

www.genesisland.co.il

Nahal Og

Nahal Og: Only 40 minutes from Jerusalem, this beautiful desert landscape offers a hiking opportunity for families. It is dry in the summer, yet the canyons provide shade for part of this hike. It is a loop and takes under 2 hours to complete. The hike is fun and challenging for older children and teens. You must be able to climb up ladder rungs drilled into the mountain.

Drive to Kibbutz Almog. *Do not go into the kibbutz.* Continue a little farther on the dirt road where there is a place to park. Enter the canyon near the gate that prevents vehicles from going down. Look for the green trail marker to begin.

ATV Riding

Trektoron Action ATV Riding: Take a one-, two- or four-hour tour of the desert. One hour is a taste of the desert. Two hours takes you into the heart of the desert, and four hours adds a refreshing dip in a desert spring. You must have a driver's license to drive, but each driver can take additional passengers.

Kfar Adumim gas station   052-868-8885, 02-535-3840

www.traktoronim.com/jerusalematvtours.html

Tel Aviv

Independence Hall

Independence Hall: Located on the historic Rothschild Boulevard in Tel Aviv, this sight is best known as the site of the signing of the Israeli Declaration of Independence. It has exhibits on the signing of the Declaration, and the history of Tel Aviv. You can listen to the original recording of the ceremony and review a brief film about the events of the period and history of the building.

16 Rothschild Blvd.   03-510-6426, 03-517-3942

Sarona: Right in the heart of Tel Aviv is a small green oasis called Sarona. The Sarona complex is a large park surrounding the restored German Templar village built in 1871. Discover the charming buildings, paved squares, indoor market, lily ponds and cafés. Interesting playgrounds for children. One of the most fascinating things is a visit to the Templar Tunnel that connected the village wine cellars. During the War of Independence in 1948, these tunnels hid the few airplanes of the Israeli army! At the Visitor Center, you can pick up an English map or order a guided tour for an in-

depth exploration of the complex, including the tunnel.
    14 Aluf Albert Street, between Kaplan and HaArba Streets
    03-604-9634

Azrieli Observatory Center / Pirates Island: View the entire Gush Dan area. The observatory is on the 49th floor of the shopping center. This is a large mall with many shops and restaurants and underground parking. On the roof of the tower is a park called Pirates Island. There are plenty of activities, including bouncy castles, rides, a few small pools, slides and trampoline-bungee. Most of the activities are for 10 and under, but there is a high ropes course and bungee for slightly older children. Get there early as it gets hot and crowded in the afternoon.
    132 Menachem Begin Street   1-700-504-150
    Exit Hashalom, on Ayalon Highway   www.islandpark.co.il

Haganah Museum: Across the street from Independence Hall, this museum describes the activities of the Haganah in the efforts to get a Jewish state. It begins in 1878 with Israel's defense history, and goes through the establishment of the Haganah as a Jewish defense force in June 1920. It includes their struggles with British authorities up through the War of Independence. Excellent 3D and audiovisual displays. This building is the former home of Eliyahu Golomb, one of the founders of the Haganah who died before the creation of the State of Israel.
    23 Rothschild Blvd.   03-560-8624
                                  www.gov.il

Yitzchak Rabin Museum: Prime Minister Yitzchak Rabin was born in Jerusalem and held a top role in the Palmach underground movement. This museum has a central corridor devoted to Rabin's childhood and adult life. It is told through short videos and photographs. Several halls capture various periods of Israeli history. The tour, which includes headsets, begins with footage of the peace rally Rabin attended the night he was assassinated, November 4th, 1995. Recommended for children 12 and older, who are interested in the recent history of the state of Israel.
    8 Chaim Levanon Street   03-745-3333
                                  www.rabincenter.org.il

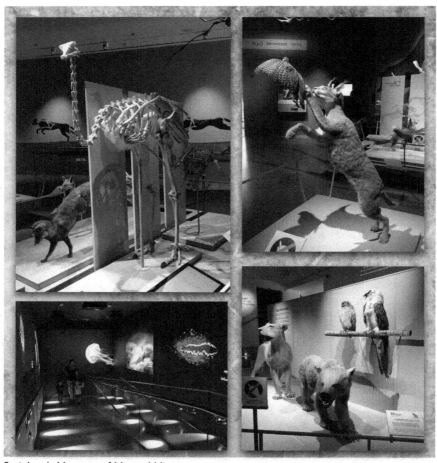

Steinhardt Museum of Natural History

Steinhardt Museum of Natural History: This state-of-the-art museum opened in July 2018. What sets it apart from other natural history museums is the emphasis on flora and fauna in Israel and the Middle East. It contains a rich collection of animal specimens as well as a room with live insects. Exhibits are interactive and teach about man's influence on nature. It takes about 2 hours to tour. Highly recommended for the entire family. They limit the number of people per day, so reserve tickets online. Great underground parking.

12 Klausner Street, Ramat Aviv (directly across from Beit Hatfuzot)
073-380-2000   www.smnh.tau.ac.il

Nahalat Binyamin: On Tuesday and Friday, a street fair takes places along this street, featuring the works of many creative artisans. All the works are original and handmade. It is adjacent to Shuk HaCarmel, and the street is named for the father of Zionism, Binyamin Ze'ev (aka Theodor) Herzl.

Nahalat Binyamin Street off Allenby Street

Palmach Museum: This museum is unlike any other you have visited. There are no documents or exhibits. Instead, the tour is carried out through experiential three-dimensional sets, background films and other various effects. A fascinating account of a personal story of young members of the Palmach is presented throughout the tour. The Palmach was the elite fighting force of the Haganah, the underground military organization of the Jewish community prior to the establishment of the State of Israel. Groups of 25 are taken through the museum, and the tour lasts about 90 minutes. The presentation is in Hebrew, but headphones are provided for English translation. Visitors must be at least 6 years old.

Ramat-Aviv   03-545-9800
10 Chaim Levanon Street   www.palmach.org.il

Eretz Israel Museum: Several pavilions spread over the vast grounds of this museum. Each pavilion is dedicated to a different cultural theme. Active exhibits include working reconstructions of ancient production methods such as glassblowing and weaving. There is a blacksmith and a craftsmen's bazaar where you can watch artisans demonstrate their techniques. There is a planetarium and nice gift shop. In the center of the museum stands Tel Qasile, an ancient archeological mound dating from the twelfth century BCE. Youth activities take place at different times of the year. Call for details.

Ramat Aviv   03-641-5244
2 Chaim Levanon Street   www.eretzmuseum.org.il

Beit Hatfutsot, Museum of the Jewish People (formerly the Diaspora Museum): This museum has been modernized. The exhibitions are innovative and interesting. At press time only three major exhibits were open; the rest is under construction and due to open in 2020. That being said, it is still a worthwhile trip. There is a Jewish humor exhibit, model synagogues from around the world and a wonderful children's exhibit on Jewish heroes. This exhibit is labeled for children ages 6-12, but it will be fun for all ages, even adults! It is filled with about 60 interactive games. During the summer and holidays you must reserve a time slot for the Heroes exhibit—it is extremely popular! There is also a genealogy section where families can look up names to trace their origins.

Ramat Aviv campus of Tel-Aviv University, Klausner Street.

Entrance through Matatia Gate 2.

Zoo at Ramat Gan

Safari Park: Over 1,000 animals live and wander free in this safari park. You can see hippos, zebras, rhinos, lions and ostriches, which will come right to your car window. If you don't have a car you can ride in a zoo vehicle. There is also a path to see many other animals. Electric golf carts are available for rent making the traditional zoo experience very enjoyable.

Ramat Gan   03-6320222

www.safari.co.il

Luna Park: This is Israel's most advanced amusement park. There are many different kinds of rides suitable for different ages. A big Ferris wheel gives you a nice view of Tel Aviv. There's a rollercoaster, water ride, and rides for toddlers as well. It can be very hot during the day in the summer, but the daytime is far less crowded than the evening.

Ganei Hata'aruha   03-642-7080

                                                          www.lunapark.co.il

iSkate: Tel Aviv's first ice skating rink is located in Luna Park. It is open every afternoon and evening, even in the summer. Children 6 and up are welcome. Skates are available in sizes 28-46.

Access through Gate 8   03-641-8418

   of Luna Park   www.iskate-lunapark.co.il

Yarkon Park (Ganei Yehoshua): This park offers a large variety of activities. These include excellent playground equipment suitable for climbing; bike rentals (including family bikes); and boat rides (rowboats, paddle boats and motor boats).

General info: 03-642-2828   Bicycles: 03-642-5286

Boat Rides: 03-642-0541

Tel Aviv's Hot Air Balloon Experience: Hover over Tel Aviv in a hot air balloon! The balloon carries up to 30 passengers and the duration of the flight is approximately 15 minutes, including takeoff and landing. There is no age requirement, but children under 14 must be accompanied by an adult.

Ganei Yehoshua/Yarkon Park   03-558-9722

                                                          www.tlv-balloon.co.il

Golfitek: Nice miniature golfing.

Ganei Yehoshua/Yarkon Park   03-699-0229

Meymadion Water Park: This water park has a wide variety of slides, fast and slow tube lanes, kiddie pools and a great wave pool. There is a large grassy area to sit and spend the day.

Ganei Yehoshua/Yarkon Park   03-642-2777

Rokach Boulevard   www.meymadion.co.il

Across from Luna Park

Coco Cola Factory

Coca Cola Factory Tour: This is Coca Cola's new virtual factory tour. It includes several halls with light, sound and interactive games and activities. This is a very professional and well-organized tour with free samples and photographs at the end of the tour. It is open year round. You must be at least 7 to visit, and no credit cards are accepted. Reservations required.

B'nei Brak   1-800-596-596, 03-671-2226

129 Rehov Kahaneman   www.cocacola.co.il

ToMoCandy Workshop

ToMoCandy Workshop: Learn to make lollipops and hard candies in this master class workshop. The candy is kosher and natural. The workshop includes a brief education on where the flavoring comes from and then a hands-on experience making the candy. Take home some beautiful products. The workshop lasts about 2 hours. It is strictly for 6 and up, as you will be around hot liquids. Gloves and aprons are provided. Lots of fun!

Ramat Gan

43 Haroe Street

052-546 8920

www.tomocandy.com

Old Jaffa: This is one of the most interesting places to tour in Tel Aviv-Jaffa. It is characterized by beautiful stone buildings, winding alleys, a fisherman's port, artists' quarter, cafés, shops and restaurants. In the center of the area is the Clock Tower, a traditional starting point for tours of the city. You can take a stroll along the sea wall or take a boat ride from the port along the coast of Tel Aviv for only about 15 NIS.

Old Jaffa

Segways Tel Aviv: A great way to discover cities. This Segway company offers tours in Tel Aviv as well as several other cities such as Haifa, Caesaria, Zichron Ya'acov and Ashdod. Begin with a 15-minute training session. Tours last about 2 hours.

03-955-0405   www.segs.co.il

Around Tel Aviv

Yaacov Agam Art Museum

Yaacov Agam Museum of Art: This museum that opened in January 2018 displays dozens of Yaacov Agam's works. The colorful and dynamic works will grab children and adults alike. Agam was born in 1928 in Rishon LeZion. He studied at the Bezalel School of Art in Jerusalem before going to Zurich and Paris to study. His works are displayed all around the world. A private tour is offered which I highly recommend.

Rishon LeZion   03-555-5900
1 Meishar St.

Rishon LeZion Open Museum: The exhibits here relate to the history of Rishon LeZion from its inception in 1882. Exhibits include lifelike mannequins, and a replica of a classroom from the first Hebrew-speaking school in the world. Touch old farming tools, and visit the Village Well to see a unique light and sound show. Children can dress up as a pioneer or pupil and take a photo.

Rishon LeZion	03-959-8862
2 Ehad Ha'am Street	03-959-8890
Kikar Hameyasdim	www.museumsinisrael.gov.il

Superland: In the heart of Rishon LeZion is an amusement park for children of all ages. There are carousels, a Ferris wheel and boat rides for very young children. There are more advanced rides and games for older children and teens, including three roller coasters. At night everything is lighted and flashing with lots of color. The park is only open on Saturdays during the school year, but it is open every day in the summer and on holidays.

Rishon LeZion	03-642-7080, 03-961-9065
5 Maryland Street	www.superland.co.il

Tnuva Factory Tour: At the Tnuva Visitors' Center you can see a virtual movie about the food we eat from the time the eggs are laid and cows are milked until it reaches your mouth. Samples and hands-on activities are included on this tour. Everything is in Hebrew however, so bring along someone who can translate for you. You must be 5 years of age to participate.

Rechovot	03-698-6250
	www.visit-tnuva.co.il

Ayalon Institute: In 1946 this kibbutz settlement hid an underground bullet factory, making bullets for Sten submachine guns. To cover the noise, a bakery and laundry were built above the factory. The entrances were concealed by a moveable oven and clothes dryer. Visitors can walk through the bakery and descend 28 steps to the bullet factory, which has been well preserved. Ask for a guided tour and movie in English in advance. You can also purchase a bullet to wear around your neck. It makes a great souvenir!

Rechovot	08-9406552
1 David Fikes Street	ayalon@shimur.org.il

Clore Garden of Science at the Weizmann Institute of Science: An entirely outdoor science museum. Children are able to experience science through interactive exhibits. Elements such as wind, sunlight and water are an integral part of many of the hands-on displays. Fascinating, innovative and fun. Guided tours are available with English speaking guides. Experience it with a guide or without, but the guides are very helpful.

Rehovot   08-937-8300

davidson.weizmann.ac.il/en/garden-of-science

Neot Kedumim, Sukkah in a tree at Neot Kedumim

Neot Kedumim, a Bible Landscape Reserve: This botanical preserve was created to display the landscapes and flora of ancient Israel. You will see trees with pomegranates, etrogim, almonds and grapes. There is a section of the reserve with all of the Sukkot (huts) described in the Mishna. You can enter many of them, including a double-decker and a sukkah built in a tree. There are self-guided tours, but the English-speaking guides give great family tours, which include activities for children at the wine press, olive press and threshing floor.

Ben Shemen   08-977-0777

        www.neot-kedumim.org.il

Meshek Muslow Farm: See, taste and learn at this working farm. Tour the animal pen with sheep, goats, turkeys, chickens and more. Walk in the fields and learn about *orla*. Learn about the four species used for Sukkot. Choose an activity that is right for your family. Pick citrus fruits, make juice, pick pomegranates—depending on the season.

Beit Gamliel (between Rechovot and Yavne)

16 HaGefen Street   054-423-3129

www.visitmeshekmuslow.com

Afrikef-Monkey Park

Afrikef-Monkey Park: This park offers guided tours, but you can walk around on your own. Signs are all in Hebrew, but you can get an English brochure at the entrance with descriptions of the monkeys there. The park hosts a wide variety of monkeys, but the most unique aspect of the park is the cage you can enter where the monkeys roam freely. There is a petting zoo and pony rides. There is also a large climbing facility for children to play on.

Ben Shemen Interchange toward Kfar Daniel off the Tel Aviv-Jerusalem highway
08-928-5888

Tuti Gil: This is a family-run organic strawberry plant. A free tour is included. You can eat as much as you want, and baskets are available at an extra cost. From December to June.

Moshav Petachia (about 20 minutes from Modin)
072-331-9847, 050-461-4406

Holon

Israel Children's Museum—Blind Museum: The exhibits in this museum encourage children to touch objects, feel textures, and basically interact with the exhibits. One of the main exhibits is "Dialogue in the Dark." A guide will lead you through a hall of darkness where you have only your other senses to rely on. You hear sounds, smell a variety of smells and touch many objects. It is an amazing experience and lasts one hour. Children must be at least 9 years old and not afraid of the dark.

    Peres Park   03-650-3010, 03-559-2080
    1 Mifraz Shlomo St.   www.childrensmuseum.org.il

Deaf Museum: Another interactive exhibit is "Invitation to Silence." A deaf guide will take you through the exhibition, which focuses on non-oral communication. Throughout this experience you will not speak or hear; instead you will discover new means of communication through hand movements and body language. The minimum age for this experience is 9. There is a program for ages 5-8 called "The Magic Forest." This is also a hands-on experience.

    Peres Park   03-650-3010, 03-559-2080
    1 Mifraz Shlomo St.   www.childrensmuseum.org.il

Yamit 2000 Water Park: This amazing water park has a number of pools and activities to enjoy, including heated and covered wave pools. There are a few fast extreme slides as well as a spa and sports center. There are also attractions designed for children ages 1-12. This park operates year-round.

    66 Mifraz Shlomo Street   www.yamit2000.co.il
    03-650-6500

Ice Peaks Holon: Nice place to skate during the hot Israeli summer. It is not too crowded, and it is usually well maintained. Skates for rent, but bring socks and warm clothing.

    Mifrats Shloo Street (located in Sportek)
    03-532-3008   www.icepeaks.co.il

Michal Negrin Factory

Michal Negrin Factory Tour: The visit to this factory includes a film presenting Michal's life journey and a guided tour of the art departments: jewelry, fashion and home décor. Her exclusive pieces of art are presented along with her personal collection and various items for sale. The gallery is magnificent. You must book in advance.

Bat Yam	03-555-3326
7 Kaf Tet BeNovember	www.michalnegrin.com

Bamba Factory tour: You can schedule a family tour at the Givon Visitor Center. Learn how the famous Israeli snack Bamba originated, watch a movie and see the assembly line. Finally have a taste of Bamba straight from the oven. This is where they produce Bamba, Popco, and other Israeli snack foods. Reservations are necessary far in advance. The tour is for children 5 and up.

Holon Industrial Zone   03-559-3024,
55 Hamelacha Street   1-700-707-676
                                           www.osem.co.il

Egged Museum: More than 60 buses are on display here. This museum offers the history of public transportation beginning with British Army surplus trucks to modern buses of today. It is primarily open for groups.

Moshe Dyan Street   03-914-2361, 03-914-2364
www.egged.co.il/Historical-Center.aspx

Ramla

Pool of the Arches

Pool of the Arches (Brachat Hakeshtot, St. Helen's Pool): Take a 30-minute stop here. This well preserved underground cistern was built during the reign of Caliph Horoun al-Rashid in 789 CE. It was erected to ensure a permanent supply of water for the residents of Ramla. A metal staircase leads down into the pool and rowboats are available to row in and out of the arches. It is a spectacular example of Islamic architecture and kids will love the rowboats in the underground pool.

Hagana Street opposite the park,   08-921-6873
    off Hertzl Street   bit.ly/tyk2ramlapool

Northern Coast and Western Galilee

Rosh Hanikra

Caption Rosh Hanikra

Rosh Hanikra: Take a two-minute cable car ride down to grottoes with a stunning view of the coast. The caves have been carved out by waves pounding on the soft, chalk rock for many years. Huge waves burst into the caves for your viewing pleasure (behind protective rails).

7 km north of Nahariya   04-985-7109

www.rosh-hanikra.com

Kayaking in Rosh Hanikra: There are now several opportunities to kayak to the grottoes. The trips leave from Betzet Beach. The round trip is about 2 hours. For ages 10 and up.

www.Kayaktours.co.il 050-865-0705   www.bgalil.co.il 052-379-8610
www.Israel-extreme.com 04-666-9898, 052-647-8474

Ma'arot Keshet

Ma'arot Keshet (Rainbow Cave): Rainbow Cave is located on the northern ridge of Nahal Betzet, overlooking Betzet creek. The ceiling of the cave collapsed leaving only an arch. You can access it from a well paved path to the parking lot. You can step out onto the arch and get a breathtaking panoramic view of the entire Western Galil. It is a favorite site for rappelling.

8km east of Rosh Hanikra, accessed from the road to Adamit

Akko

Old City of Akko: This is a 4,000-year-old city. Walk the ancient port, the former capital of the Crusader kingdom of Acre. See the castle, Templar tunnel and the largest prison from the time of the British Mandate. Headphones are available for a better understanding of the sights. It is best to go to the visitors' center first.

Old Acre   1-700-708020
1 Weizmann Street   www.akko.org.il

Boat Rides in Akko: Boat rides in Akko give a view of how the ancient coastal city appeared to seafaring vessels in previous generations. Boats hold up to 25 passengers and the music varies depending on the crowd. The ride lasts about 25 minutes and passes the lighthouse and offers a great view of the city walls. There are cruising type boats and speed boats as well. Just walk up to the pier and see what's available.

Marina at the southern end of the Old City

Or Torah Synagogue: This Tunisian Synagogue is one of a kind. It is covered in mosaics inside and out. The mosaics and stained-glass windows depict the history of the Jewish people and the Land of Israel. Schedule your visit in advance. This is not specifically for children, but it is worth a visit.

13 Eliezer Kaplan Street   04-981-8451

Lochamei Hageta'ot (Ghetto Fighters Museum): This is a Holocaust museum with excellent photographs, a model of the Anne Frank House in Amsterdam, a model of a camp, and many other exhibits. There is a Children's Memorial dedicated to the one-and-a-half million children who died in the Holocaust. This museum is designed for children to begin to understand the events of the Holocaust without showing shocking images.

2 km north of Akko   04-995-8080
                                  www.gfh.org.il

Haifa

Bahá'í Gardens

Bahá'í Gardens: This is one of the most popular sites in the Middle East, located in the heart of Haifa. The gardens offer graveled paths, hedges and beautiful flower beds constantly groomed by gardeners. The gardens are comprised of a staircase of 18 terraces extending up the Northern slope of Mount Carmel. At the heart is the golden-domed Shrine of the Báb. Modest clothing and long pants for men are required.

80 Hatzionut Ave.   04-835-8358

www.bahaipictures.com

National Museum of Science, Technology and Space: Children and adults will love this hands-on museum. The excellent exhibits, educational games and puzzles are good for all ages. Included is a fighter jet where you can step into the cockpit. The newest addition to this museum is a 4D interactive cinematrix theater, which engages all your senses simultaneously. You see, hear, feel and ride in this experience. It is complemented by scent, air flow and water effects. English available through advanced booking. You must be 6 and older for the film.

    12 Balfour Street   04-861-4444
                                             www.madatech.org.il

Doll Museum: This special museum takes you through the history of the Jewish people with dioramas and almost 1,000 lifelike models. Children who love dolls will really enjoy this museum and they will learn something at the same time.

    Castra Shopping Mall (south entrance)
    8 Flieman Street   04-859-0001

Israel Railway Museum: This museum illustrates the development of rail transport in Israel since 1892. This site is actually an operating railway station, which enhances its atmosphere. You can board many of the trains, including one used by dignitaries such as Winston Churchill and David Ben Gurion.

    Haifa East Station   04-856-4293
                                             www.rail.co.il

National Maritime Museum: 5,000 years of maritime history can be found in this museum. There are model ships, coins and underwater finds from nearby shipwrecks.

    198 Allenby Road   04-853-6622
                                             www.nmm.org.il

Ha'Em Garden (Park, Zoo and Nature Museum): This park hosts a small natural forest, an amusement park, Haifa's educational zoo, and a nature museum.

    122 HaNasi Blvd.   04-837-2231, 04-837-6861
                                             www.carmelithaifa.com

Hanging Bridge, Nesher Park

Nesher Park: Two hanging bridges make this Keren Kayemet park a special visit. The bridges are accessible with just a 10-minute walk along a flat path. The bridges offer beautiful views and are safe to cross. You will probably not enjoy these bridges if you have a fear of heights. There are hiking trails to enjoy, and a nice playground for children. This park is easily reachable from anywhere in the Haifa area.

Nesher Park   www.kkl-jnf.org
HeHaruv Street

The Carmelite: This is the only underground train in Israel. It has six stations, and escalators lead up and down to the subway. The last station brings you to Ha'Em Park. If you are up for some exercise you can walk down the 1,000 steps leading from the station to the Lower City.

First Station is opposite the port beside HaAtzmaut Street
04-833-5970
www.urbanrail.net/as/hai/haifa.htm

Haifa Cable Car: Get a great aerial view in Haifa's cable car. This is a fast way to get up or down the side of the mountain. It travels from the beach at the western end of Bat Galim to the tip of Mt. Carmel.

04-833-5970   cablecar-haifa.co.il/

Xpark (Challenge Park): This is one of the largest challenge parks in Israel. There are activities for children of all ages. Challenges include a rope bridge park, a rock climbing wall, a zip line , and paintball. For the younger members of the family there is a low ropes course, ball pit and inflatables.

Mercaz Congressim, off Route 4.   1-599-524-400
                                         www.xpark.co.il

South of Haifa

Atlit Detainee Museum: You will have a better appreciation of what Jews sacrificed to reach their homeland after this visit. This was the largest detention camp opened by the authorities of the British Mandate to hold Jewish immigrants who exceeded the annual quota. It is impressive and portrays an important aspect of Israel's modern history. When you first enter the camp you will see a double wire fence, and then a large building. This is where the men and women were separated, and their clothing taken, before they were sent to the showers. Entering the large building you can see the showers and a turntable on which clothes were put for delousing. Down by the sea is a large ship with audiovisual presentations that children and adults of all ages will enjoy.

> Off Route 2 to Route 7110,   04-984-1980
>   south of Haifa

Dag-bakfar: In this park the theme is "Give a man a fish you give him one meal; teach him how to fish and you give him a meal for life." Here you can rent equipment and spend a relaxing day fishing. There are picnic areas and grills available to cook your fish at the end of the day.

> Yokneam   04-989-4095, 04-959-0328
>   www.dag-bakfar.com

Park Balagan: This park is for children up to 13 years old. It includes inflatable rides, electric bikes, a pool with moving boats, a train, table football and much more.

> Kibbutz Yagur   04-984-8989
>   www.ba-lagan.co.il (Hebrew only)

Zichron Yaakov

Beit Aaronson: This museum was once the home of Aaron Aaronson (1876-1919), famous for discovering the predecessor to modern wheat. However, he and his sisters became local heroes as leaders of a spy ring called the NILI, a group dedicated to ousting the Turks from Palestine. They worked with the British during World War I. The house remains as it was and includes the secret hiding place where Sarah Aaronson's gun was stored. She used it to commit suicide to escape her captors. An interesting movie tells the story and an English guided tour can be requested. Hours end early.

40 Hameyasdim Street   04-639-0120
www.nili-museum.org.il

Tut-Neyar Paper Mill: The primary purpose of this mill is to produce handmade paper. The results are beautiful. You can watch the paper being made and arrange for a paper-making workshop for your family if you call ahead. It takes about two hours and is best for children 5 and up. You can purchase paper and other products as well.

39 Hamayesdim   54-649-0559
www.tutneyar.co.il

Carmel Winery: Learn about the winery, built in 1892 by Baron Edmond de Rothschild. It is the largest winery in Israel. Here you can see the new and ancient worlds of winemaking in one setting. Tasting is part of the tour. There is also a restaurant on the premises.

Derech Hayekev (Winery Street)   04-639-1788, 04-629-0977
www.carmelwines.co.il

Tishbi Winery: One of the most esteemed wineries in Israel, with a very personal touch. The Visitors Center offers gourmet chocolate and wine tasting. Call ahead to reserve a winery tour.

Binyamina   04-638-0434
www.tishbi.com

Park Alona

Park Alona: Guided tours are given, similar to Siloan Pool in Jerusalem. However, these tunnels are wider, taller and better lit, making it less claustrophobic and easier to traverse with children. The tour only lasts about 20 minutes and there is an escape route up a flight of stairs if needed for a young child. It may have been a source of water for Caesaria and connected to the aqueducts there. It's a great way to spend a warm afternoon.

Located off Route 4 between Moshav Amikam and Bat Shlomo,
near Binyaminaband
04-638-8622   www.meykedem.com

Ramat Hanadiv Memorial Gardens: The gardens are beautiful, and the surrounding nature reserve is great for hikers. The gardens include the crypt of Baron and Baroness Rothschild, the Fragrance Garden where you are encouraged to smell and touch the plants, the Rose Garden with fountains representing the Rothschild family members, the Palm Garden, and an observation point with a beautiful view.

Route #652   06-639-7726
                                         www.ramat-hanadiv.org.il

Aviation Gallery at Paradive: Dan Mokady, a former fighter pilot, relays stories about the first European aviators to land in Israel. He has a collection of vintage aircraft. The collection includes a Czech Mig, French-made Dornier planes that formed Israel's earliest air force, and a 1940 Tiger Moth biplane. You can see the collection of planes at Mokady's skydiving business called Paradive.

Habonim Beach   04-639-1068
                                       www.paradive.co.il

Tomcars

Tom Cars/Riding Stables in Beit Oren: Teens with a license or permit can drive a four-wheeled ATV with a guide through beautiful fields and dirt roads. Three additional passengers can ride in each vehicle. Kids will love this experience! You can also do some horseback riding, rappelling and zip lining.

Kibbutz Beit Oren   04-830-7444, 077-230-6340
                                       www.carmelim.org.il

Dor Marine Tour

Dor Marine Tour/Nachsholim: Explore the revival of *tekhelet*. This is the site of an ancient Roman port where the remains of an ancient Roman dye house were uncovered. Learn about tekhelet from an audiovisual presentation. Then enjoy snorkeling in the Mediterranean and explore the snail habitat. Dye and process wool and discuss the religious uses of tekhelet. Allow 3–4 hours. Bring water shoes, a towel and bathing suit. Women please bring an extra t-shirt for snorkeling. Reservations a must!

   Chof Dor/Nachsholim, access from Highway #4. Turn at sign for Dor/Nachsholim.
   Follow the road until the parking lot.
02-590-0577   www.tekhelet.com

Daliyat El Carmel: This is Israel's largest Druze village. The Druze who live here serve in the Israeli army. The attraction here is the shuk, or marketplace. The shops sell rugs, handwoven baskets, pottery, tablecloths, backgammon games and so much more. Kids will enjoy the shuk experience.

   South of Haifa on Route 672

Caves at Nahal Me'arot Nature Reserve: You can visit three prehistoric caves. They are up a steep flight of stairs on a fossil reef that was covered by the sea 100 million years ago. Inside one of the caves is an audiovisual show on how early man lived. There is also a display on the daily life of early man and a skeleton on the premises.

   3 km south of Ein Hod, I km east of Route 4
   04-984-1750, 04-984-1752   bit.ly/tyk2mearot

Ein Hod: 150 artists and their families live and work in this lovely village. There are many galleries to visit, with the Central Art Gallery in the heart of the village. Watch an artist at work, or try creating something at one of the workshops. Visits should be arranged in advance, otherwise you may be disappointed, as many of them are not open all the time. Our favorite is Naomi and Zeev Pottery. You can take a lesson on working the ceramic wheel, or make whistles from clay. Children love this. Their numbers are 04-984-1107, 050-775-7142

Ein Hod   054-481-1968
                                               www.ein-hod.info

Caesarea

Caesarea

Caesarea National Park: Once the largest city in Judea, now an extensive archeological site. You can see the Crusader City, with its large moat, bridge and tower; the restored Roman Amphitheater, now used for concerts; and the Hippodrome, a horse racing arena. Herod built a port here still visible from a boat, though most of it is now underwater. Rabbi Akiva and other Jewish martyrs were tortured here after the Bar Kochba Revolt. While this site was great when it was mostly ruins, they now have quite a unique multimedia presentation for all family members. You can [virtually] speak to and ask questions of several famous historic figures such as Rabbi Akiva, and view an excellent film which shows you what Caesarea looked like at the time of King Herod, and in various eras after that. Combine this with a boat ride (see Kef Yam) and it makes for an excellent trip.

04-626-8823, 04-636-1358

Speed boat, Kef Yam

bit.ly/tyk2caesarea

Kef Yam: Ride on a speed boat if you like action or on a glass-bottom boat if you prefer a more leisurely ride. It is possible to view many of the sites from this angle, often a more interesting way for children to do the viewing, especially on a hot day. Excellent view of Herod's harbor.

Sdot Yam   04-636 4444

Orange Picking: Orange and citrus fruit picking in a family grove. Pick delicious fruit, have a picnic and squeeze your own juices.

Moshav Bitan Aharon   052-884-1629

Strawberry Picking: Strawberries are available to pick from December to June.

Kibbutz Mishmar HaSharon   www.sadot.biz
052-595-6654

Kibbutz Ein Shemer: This kibbutz is famous for The Old Courtyard. It offers a variety of activities and a small museum where you can learn about the life of the early pioneers. You can bake rolls in the restored flour mill, take a tour on a tractor, or ride a restored 1915 Turkish train. Its newest attraction is a reconstructed oil press from the early 20th century. Pricing is based on the number of activities you choose.

Route 65, turn south at the Menashe junction

06-637-4327   www.courtyard.co.il

Clementine picking: With the cost of entry you can fill a bag with up to 2kg of clementines that you pick yourself.

Kefar Netter   052-977-0490

                                         www.hakatif.com

Netanya

Netanya

Netanya Beaches and Resort Town: Netanya has some of the most beautiful beaches in Israel. It is built on a cliff, and therefore its beaches are many steps down; however in the center of town, there is a large outdoor elevator down to the Sironit beach. At the bottom, the breakers keep the waves to a mild roar, lounge chairs are available to rent, and water sports are also available. At present there is also a kosher restaurant on the beach. The promenade along the beach stretches for miles and is a great place for a walk. There are many small playgrounds along the way. The pedestrian square (Kikar Haazmaut) hosts a variety of restaurants and vendors in the evenings. An artistic fountain synchronizes with music and has a water screen with holograms. There is a large blow-up panda for children to jump on for a small fee, and sometimes, there are small rides for children in the square. If you want a day off to relax and just visit the beach, this is a great place to do it!

www.netanya.muni.il

Paragliding in Netanya: Netanya's beach-front cliffs make for a great place to launch paragliders—light aircraft that soar on the air currents. Because a trained instructor controls the craft, a child as young as five can fly along. There are several paragliding firms licensed by Netanya along the waterfront. The paragliding season is from April to October. Several of these companies also offer paragliding in other locations throughout Israel, balloon rides, and other aviation activities. It's best to call ahead to reserve a spot in advance, and availability is subject to change if the wrong weather blows in. The experience of floating in the air is incredible, but not cheap: Budget at least $50 for a ten minute ride.

Dekel Paragliding: 03-506-0063, 052-257-8645, www.gliding.co.il

Dvir Paragliding: 054-655-4466/77, dvirparagliding.co.il

Israglide: 052-803-3824, www.israglide.com

Point of View: 052-525-7541, www.fly-pov.co.il

Planetanya: A new planetarium in Netanya offers incredible planetarium films as well as lectures and hands-on activities. Most of it is offered in Hebrew but English can be arranged. There is an area with shade outdoors for children. You should plan on at least 2-3 hours here for the movie and a hands-on activity.

168 Ben Gurion Street   09-748-5760

www.planetanya.org.il

The Ranch, horseback riding

Horseback Riding: If you want to try some horseback riding, northern Netanya is the place to do it. It's good for families and beginners as well as seasoned riders. You cannot beat the scenery—the ride is mostly along the beach.

The Ranch: Call for reservations.
Netanya coast road
09-866-3525
www.the-ranch.co.il

The Cactus Ranch:
050-699-9000
www.cactus4u.biz

Netanya Museum: An innovative exhibit for the whole family. The display tracks the history of the city from its founding in 1929. The exhibit is in just one room and the information is in Hebrew, but you can get an English speaking guide and an English brochure which explains everything.

3 McDonald Street

09-884-0020
www.netanya.muni.il

Go Karting Poleg

Go Karting Poleg, Netanya: Go-karting is officially for ages 13 and up, but exceptions are sometimes made for children a bit younger. The program begins with a short lesson on signs, symbols and safety. Then you get your helmet and buckle up for a race around the indoor track. Each lap is officially timed. Bystanders can watch the lap times on a television screen while they watch the race. Everyone gets a printout of their race stats. Allow one hour. Great fun for teens. Call for reservations.

Azor Tassiah, Poleg   09-885-4477

24 Giborei Israel   www.gokarting.co.il

Adventure Playground at Winter Pond Park: This is a unique playground, equipped with bridges, ladders, slides, seesaws, and a carousel.

Ben Gurion Boulevard

(enter Netanya from the southern exit and drive about 500 meters. Turn right into Winter Pond Park)

Parrot Farm, Kfar Hess

Havat Hatukim (Parrot Farm): This farm hosts hundreds of beautiful birds. They're hand-raised, so you can hold many of them. There is also a large petting farm with rabbits, goats, ducks and more.

Kfar Hess	09-796-1773
	www.havat-hatukim.co.il

Skimulater: These indoor ski simulator centers offer skiers of all skills levels an opportunity to improve their skiing. There are three centers, all of which work together. Emek Hefer is the reservation center for all three.

Emek Hefer industrial area	04-622-2055
Holon industrial area	www.skimulator.co.il
Haifa	

Ga'ash Golf Course: Nine-hole golf course, open year-round.

Kibbutz Gaash	09-951-5111
	www.golfgaash.co.il

Tractor Museum

Tractor Museum: This amazing collection of tractors is another hidden gem. In addition to hundreds of tractors, this museum tells the story of the first agricultural settlements in Israel, through collected artifacts from every walk of life. They have tools, kitchen equipment, toys, a dental office and so much more. Enjoyable for all ages!

Ein Vered   052-2452457

tractor.org.il

Shefayim Water Park: Nice, clean water park with a variety of slides, kiddie pools, swimming pool and a wave pool.

Kibbutz Shefayim, off Route 2 outside   09-959-5756
Netanya   www.waterpark.co.il

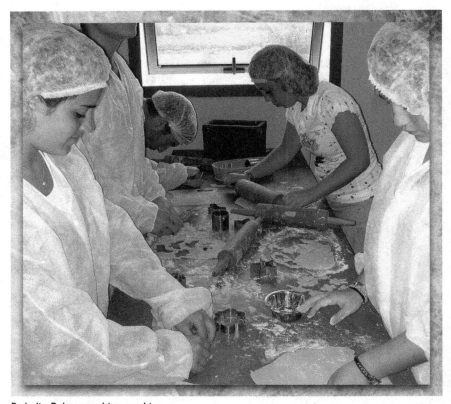

Roladin Bakery, making cookies

Roladin Bakery: This tour is a must-do. The guide will take you to watch the bakers in action. Then you will go to a room complete with rolling pins and fresh dough. Everyone gets to design their own cookies, and then watch a movie about the production of Roladin products while the cookies bake. The bakery also has an excellent café for a dairy lunch. Reservations for the tour are a must!

Kadima, just south of Netanya   054-257-6885
                                            www.roladin.co.il

Soos Va'Agala

Soos Va'Agala: Wooden toys workshop—Spend quality time together with your children working on a wooden toy of your choice. For children ages 4–13. The workshop lasts 2-3 hours. Build and paint your toy. The cost is $40-$80 depending on your choice of toy. Call in advance. Immediately outside the workshop is the world's largest rocking horse, which is in the Guinness Book of World Records. If it's summer, be sure to taste the grapes on your way out!

15 Hehadar Street, Kadima   09-899-0909, 054-471-7286
                                             www.soosagala.co.il

Utopia Park

Utopia Park: Families can wander in a jungle environment between waterfalls, fish pools and tropical plants. Attractions include a park with carnivorous plants, a butterfly garden, two plant mazes, and thousands of orchids. There is a wide variety of animals including birds, deer, sheep, and peacocks. There is something for everyone in the family here. The park is open year-round.

Kibbutz Bahan, Emek Hefer

Off Route 57 between Route 4 and Route 6

From Netanya, turn left at Nitzane intersection

09-878-2191   www.utopiapark.co.il

Alexander Stream, Turtle Park,: This is one of the nicest streams in central Israel. You can park at Yannai beach and take a lovely hike here, about 4 km crossing over Turtle Bridge to Turtle Park; or you can park by Turtle Park and just visit here. You can see huge turtles, catfish, geese and otters.

Hof Bet Yanai National Park   bit.ly/tyk2hof

Hadov Halavan (The White Bear): This indoor climbing center is a huge hit with kids of all ages. Older children will enjoy bungee jumping, trampolines, indoor rappelling, rope walking and wall climbing. There are many activities for young children as well. In the summer there are also water activities. Fifteen minutes north of Netanya.

Emek Hefer   04-689-6078
21 Tzvi HaNahal   www.wbear.co.il

Herzliya

Appolonia National Park

Apollonia National Park: This site is located on a cliff in Herzliya. Remains of settlements that existed here date back 1,800 years. You can see a moat from the time of the Crusades, water reservoirs from the Byzantine period, and remains of stoves, halls and courtyards. What kids usually find the most interesting are the ballista stones that Crusader soldiers shot at the Mameluke soldiers, stored in huge piles in the Burnt Room. There are clear explanations next to each area, with cartoon style posters to spark the imagination. Never crowded, and worth seeing if you aren't "ruined" out.

Hertzliya   09-955-0929

bit.ly/tyk2apollonia

Raanana

Raanana Park: This is one of the largest parks in the Sharon area. It is a great place for some rest and relaxation. The park offers a large playground for children with swings, carousels, slides and climbing equipment. There is a zoological garden where children are invited to visit the petting corner, and plenty of shaded walking paths along the lake. There is also a train for young children which travels around the park.

Yerushalayim Street across from Beit Levinstein Hospital

Leket Israel: This organization provides food to soup kitchens, homeless shelters and other social service organizations in Israel. People can participate by joining Leket in the fields to harvest various fruits and vegetables in different parts of the country. Call them to see where they are harvesting. You can also help sort and pack the food at the logistics center in Raanana.

09-790-9202   www.leket.org

Kfar Saba

Soap workshop

Soap Cake Factory: The soap cake factory offers workshops for families to make their own soaps and spa products. Choose a color, fragrance and shape! Workshops run about 2 hours. Take home some professional-looking soap! Recommended for ages 6 and up. The process requires some downtime while waiting for products to cool.

4 Ha-Khish Street   058-426-4454

www.soapcakefactory.com

Saidel's Artisan Baking Institute

Breads of the Beit Hamikdash: Saidel's Artisan Baking Institute specializes in teaching people how to bake Jewish breads. They begin with a virtual tour of the *Beit Hamikdash* followed by an explanation of the special ingredients and methods used in baking the breads. Then you get to the hands-on mixing, shaping and baking the bread, using the ancient techniques of 2,000 years ago. Allow 3 hours for the workshop.

Karnei Shomron   09-794-1222
22 Hahadas Street   www.saidels.com

Ashdod

Ashdod Yam Park: This mid-city park is clean and nicely maintained. They have regular organized activities, events, and performances. There is a playground, skate park and a man-made lake where you can rent a boat. Don't miss the musical fountain show in the evening. Free parking and a view of the ocean.

Center of Ashdod

Eye of the Sun: An artistic attraction, this is one of the city's famous monuments. It looks like a huge synthetic eye. After sunset this monument shines with various changing colored lights.

3 Har Gilboa Street

Sderot

Hesder Yeshiva

Hesder Yeshiva: Visit the yeshiva with the menorah made of Kasam Rockets. Enjoy a delicious lunch.

08-661-1360   www.sderot.org

Sderot

Town: Visit the indoor playground and the outdoor playgrounds with bomb shelters designed as part of the playground. Stop and see the beautifully painted bus stops all around the town, which are also bomb shelters. On display at the police station are many of the rockets that have fallen in town. See the scenic lookout over Gaza.

Beit Shean Area

Beit Shean National Park: Since excavations began here, dozens of layers of settlement dating back to 5,000 BCE have been revealed. Attractions at this national park include a 7,000-seat Roman theater, the amphitheater where gladiators once fought, bathhouses, temples and a *cardo* (marketplace). A multimedia night tour of the ancient city operates nine months of the year, offering visitors the opportunity to enjoy the site in the cool night air in a region known for its hot summer days. Visitors stroll through the streets of the excavated city of Scythopolis while watching audiovisual presentations projected onto dozens of giant screens on the columns and walls. Sound effects include voices, stories and music. Visitors meet "local" characters experiencing the earthquake that destroyed the city in 749 CE. Families will enjoy the experience of being transported back 2,000 years in time.

City of Beit Shean 04-648-1122

bit.ly/tyk2beit

Gan Hashlosha (Sachne): Sachne is a lovely national park with a spring that is warm year-round. There is also a river deep enough for diving in some places. It has great picnic grounds. The name is derived from the three natural springs or pools on the premises.

Beit Shean, off Route 669 04-658-6219

bit.ly/tyk2sahne

Belavoir (Kochav Hayarden): This fortress was built in 1168. This national park has a well preserved Crusader castle which includes a bridge (once a drawbridge) with a beautiful view of the Jordan valley and the Kinneret. It is worth the trip up the winding road to reach this fortress.

Route 717 turnoff 12 km north of 04-658-1766

Beit Shean bit.ly/tyk2kokhav

Huga Water Park: A little off the beaten track, this park doesn't have adventurous slides, but it does have three huge natural spring-fed lakes. There is a rope slide ride straight into the lake, and a fishing pool.

Jordan Valley 04-658-1111

Kibbutz Hamadia

Gangaroo

Gangaroo: A lovely four-acre zoo of Australian wildlife. It includes koalas, kangaroos and wallabies. There is also a petting zoo. You can enter the kangaroo compound and hop around with them—truly amazing. There's a petting zoo where you can feed Australian farm animals, including mini goats.

Off Route 669, to the left of Gan Hashlosha (Sachne)

04-648-8060   bit.ly/tyk2garoo

Reptile exhibit at Hamat Gader

Hamat Gader: Once a major spa of the Roman Empire, now a modern spa. It is built around three mineral hot springs, both indoors and out. You can also indulge in a massage. There is a children's freshwater pool with a unique water slide. Other attractions include a reptile exhibit with an alligator farm where kids can hold a baby alligator. There is a fishing pond where you can catch your own dinner. Tour the ruins of the Roman spa. You can spend a whole day here.

19 km east of Zemach junction   04-665-9999

www.hamat-gader.com

The Harod spring bubbles up from Gideon Cave at the foot of the Gilbo'a. This was the site where, according the Bible, Gideon's soldiers were tried and selected for the war against the Midianites:

"Then Jerubbaal, who is Gideon, and all the people who were with him, rose up early, and camped beside the well of Harod; so that the army of the Midianites were on their north side, by the hill of Moreh, in the valley." (Judges 7, 1)

"So he brought down the people to the water; and the Lord said to Gideon, Every one who laps the water with his tounge, like a dog laps, him shall you set by himself; likewise every one who bows down upon his knees to drink. And the number of those who lapped, putting their hand to their mouth, were three hundred men; but all the rest of the people bowed down upon their knees to drink water." (Judges 7, 6-7)

"And he divided the three hundred men into three companies, and he put a shofar in every man's hand, with empty jars, and torches inside the jars. And he said to them, Look at me and do likewise..." (Judges 7, 16-17)

The graves of Joshua Henkin, freer of lands, and his wife Olga lie above the spring.
A memorial to the valley people was built beside these graves.

עין חרוד
פטים ז' (1

לק בלשונו
יכרע על
ולוש מאות
(6,5 ז' ים

שופרות ביד
אליהם ממני

ושע חנקין.

לבני העמק.

Maayan Harod

Maayan Harod: Near Beit Shean is a beautiful park with springs running through it. Children will enjoy playing in the springs. There is a large pool with a nice playground as well.

04-653-2211   bit.ly/tyk2harod

Ski Gilboa at night

Ski Gilboa: Rent skis, boots and helmets and ski year-round at this center. There is a rope tow and a ski lift. There is no snow, but you would not guess it from watching the kids ski down the mountain. Paintball and laser tag are also available.

Har Gilboa   073-251-0000

                                    www.huga.co.il

Galita Chocolate Workshop on Kibbutz Dagania Bet: This Kibbutz is just south of the Kinneret. They offer excellent chocolate making workshops for all ages. Upon arrival you can choose which type of chocolate project you would like to make. There are projects for everyone. It is well organized and lots of fun. You will leave with lots of chocolate! There is another division of this workshop outside Jerusalem at Moshav Tzuba.

Kibbutz Dagania Bet   www.galita.co.il
04-675-5608

Kibbutz Sde Eliyahu: This religious kibbutz operates Bio-Tour experiential farm tours for the whole family. Guests learn about kibbutz life and organic farming. Tours last about 2 hours and take place early in the day or evening. You can add on a meal or hands-on activities at an additional cost. Reservations are required.

Kibbutz Sde Eliyahu   04-609-6986, 04-609-6525
                                     www.sde.org.il

Lower Galil

Bee Farm at Dvorat Hatavor

Dvorat Hatavor: Why is honey kosher? How is silk made? Learn more about both on your guided tour at this honey and silk farm. Children have the opportunity to make their own beeswax candle. Tour the silkworm building to see how silkworms are grown and find out about making silk. Your tour also includes an up-close look at beehives from behind a well fenced-in area. Dvorat Hatavor offers a shop to buy honey and a variety of honey-related products. This trip will prove to be fun and educational. For ages 3 and up. Call for visiting hours and reservations.

Moshav Shadmot Devora, off Route# 767, near Route #65

04-676-9598, 050-326-160   www.dvorat-hatavor.co.il

Mount Arbel

Hike Mount Arbel: At the time of the Hasmoneans there was a city sitting on top of this mountain, known as Arbela. There are some remains and antiquities on the mountainside to visit on your way up. This mountain provides a challenge for hikers, as it is directly up a cliff. There are hand holds and steps for climbers, but it's definitely a challenge for those with a fear of heights. At the top you are rewarded with a magnificent view of the Sea of Galilee, and views as far as Mount Hermon to the north and Mount Tavor to the south. The climb up takes about an hour. If you don't want to climb you can drive up the backside of the mountain from Moshav Arbel.

Take Highway 90 to the Bedouin village of Hamam on Road 807. The trail begins at the bottom of the slopes across from the kiosk.

Marzipan Museum: This program begins with a short, entertaining film on the making of marzipan. This is followed by a viewing of amazing sculptures made of marzipan, including everything from Biblical scenes to cartoon characters. Everyone then gets their own marzipan to make their own sculptures. Chocolate is an alternative for anyone who prefers it. Lots of fun for all.

| Sderot Kakal | 04-677-2111 |
| Kfar Tavor | www.marzifun.co.il |

Safed: Safed is filled with historical sites dating back many centuries. There is the famous mikveh, as well as the Safed Cemetery where many well-known rabbis are buried. There is a very long staircase which was used by the British to separate the Arab and Jewish quarters.

There are many well-known synagogues here, including the Ashkenazi HaAri Synagogue and the Sephardic HaAri Synagogue. The Abuhov Synagogue contains a Torah scroll from the Middle Ages and the Yosef Caro Synagogue displays the famous Shulchan Aruch.

There are many shops and art galleries on Gallery Street. A few things that may interest children are the shuk that takes place every Wednesday, the Safed Candle Shop and the HaMeiri Cheese Shop.

Our experience with Safed and children is that it is a lot of walking and sightseeing, so it is more for older children interested in synagogues and historical sites.

www.safed.co.il

Tiberias: Tiberias is the only city on the Kinneret. Moses Maimonides (Rambam) is buried here. Rambam was considered to be the greatest religious scholar of the Middle Ages. Though he never lived in Tiberias, his remains were brought here from Egypt. The tomb is located on Ben Zakkai Street.

The Maimonides Heritage Center: The Maimonides Heritage Center, located next to the Kever of the Rambam, offers you a chance to learn more about the life and works of the famous scholar, doctor and philosopher. Group programs are available by advance reservation. Call for more information. Also located in the center are escape rooms. The Maimonides Puzzle room will complete your trip. Recommended for ages 10 and up.

| 6 Hatanaim Street | 053-530-3018 |
| | www.mhcpuzzleroom.com |

The Kinneret (Sea of Galilee): This is a freshwater lake and a refreshing place to take a swim. There are several beaches, plus water activities for children. There are boat rides going from Tiberias to Ein Gev on the eastern shore (about 45 minutes each way). They leave frequently in July, August and holidays. There is a promenade with restaurants and shops along the water.

Sailing on the Kinneret: Kibbutz Ein Gev has a fleet of boats which can carry 80–165 guests to ports all around the lake. Fishing cruises are also available. Join the fishing crew for a day at work. Experience net fishing and enjoy the excitement of the chase. Cruises last about 4 hours and can take up to 7 people. For a one-hour cruise and fishing demonstration call: 054-565-8006.

> Ein Gev Harbor
> 04-665-9800; 054-565-8009 (4-hour cruise)
> www.eingev.co.il

Luna Gal Waterpark: On the Eastern side of the Kinneret (Sea of Galilee) is one of Israel's biggest water parks. It's great fun for the whole family. There is a fast Kamikaze slide, Hurricane water slides and many other attractions.

> Golan Beach, Sea of Galilee   04-667-8000
> www.dugal.co.il

Aqua Kef: A one-of-a-kind water park actually in the lake. There is a small park for children ages 3–6 and another for ages 6 and up. Buy tickets in advance for 45-minute sessions on the floating playground.

> Ganim Beach   1-700-555-079
> www.aquakef.co.il

Majrase water hike: Majrase is a great hike for young kids. You walk along the floor of a river, which is flat, not rocky, making it an easy walk for children. The river is calm and refreshing. Allow about an hour for this 2 km hike. You can reach it from Highway 92, which you take to the Northeastern part of the Kinneret. At the Ma'aleh Gamla junction you turn left in the direction of the Kinneret (if you are traveling north). Continue to Majrase Nature Reserve.

> A bit north of Kinar   04-679-3410
> bit.ly/tyk2majrase

Zaki Water Hike: This is the same entrance and river as the Majrase, but it is much more difficult. It is rocky, and the river has currents in parts of it. You must be a swimmer. Walking is more slippery. At the end there is a refreshing pool to relax in. To return to your car you must leave the river to your left and walk about 30 minutes through orchards. The trail is marked, but not always easy to find. The directions are the same as Majrase, but you continue farther into the reserve following different trail signs. You will find the beginning of Zaki when you reach a pole with a sign on it that says Zaki.

04-679-3410   bit.ly/tyk2majrase

Elite Chocolate Factory Tour: This is a great factory tour if you are able to make reservations. You must call way in advance of your trip.

Nazeret, Illit   1-800-777-7777
                                             www.elite.co.il

Tzippori National Park: Archaeologists have discovered much of the city from the Roman and Byzantine eras, and Tzippori was the capital of the Galilee during the Second Temple period. This site includes an impressive water system and fabulous mosaic floors, one which is known as the Mona Lisa of the Galilee. This will be an interesting site for children if the hands-on mosaic making is available at the time of your visit. Call for information and to schedule an activity.

Off Route 79   04-656-8272
                                             bit.ly/tyk2tzipori

Megiddo: Twenty-six layers of historical periods have been uncovered here. This is an amazing archeological site and it includes a sacrificial altar and long water tunnel. You go down many steps to walk through it, and though it no longer contains water, the air is cool, damp and refreshing on a hot day. It is also a steep climb back up. In Hebrew, Har-Megiddo became Armageddon in the New Testament, and it is thought to be the place where the forces of good and evil will battle it out in a final skirmish.

Between the Megiddo and Yokne'am Junctions, Road #66
04-659-0316   bit.ly/tyk2megiddo

Beit She'arim

Beit She'arim

Beit She'arim National Park: During the Mishnaic and Talmudic periods, this was the most prestigious burial site in the Jewish world. The Sanhedrin was based here for a time and it was also the home of Rabbi Yehuda Hanasi, chief editor of the Mishnah and leader of the Jewish community during the Roman occupation of Judea. Huge catacombs are built into and under the hills of this site. There are many chambers containing more than 200 sarcophagi. Roman and Greek symbols are carved into many of them. Eerie, yet exciting.

    20 km south of Haifa, off Route 70   04-983-1643

                                                      bit.ly/tyk2shearim

Kfar Kedem: This village is a recreated ancient Galilee village from the time of the Mishnah, with many hands-on activities. You can be a shepherd, plow fields, make pita and ride donkeys.

    Hosha'aya, Nazareth   04-656-5511

                                                   www.k-k.co.il

Yaar Kofim Monkey Farm

Yaar Kofim Monkey Farm: If your children like animals, this is the place to go. Deer, mountain goats and gazelles roam the park freely. Other animals are in cages. However, the highlight of this farm is the monkeys. You can buy food and enter the cage, which resembles their natural habitat. The monkeys will come to check you out, sit on your head and shoulders, or reach from the trees to take your food. Set a time limit—kids could spend all day here.

Yodfat, Misgav: from the south, make a left turn at the Hamovil junction to road
No. 784 toward Karmiel and Misgav. Search for the right turn to Yodfat.
04-980-1265   www.kofim.co.il

Upper Galil and Golan

Talmudic Village

Talmudic Village of Katzrin: Near the city of Katzrin is a reconstructed village that has been brought to life in the location of a village from Talmudic times. In the village you can see an ancient olive oil press, wander through a reconstructed kitchen, pantry, living room, bedroom and courtyard. Explore the remains of a Talmudic-era synagogue. Special arrangements can be made for bread-baking, pottery making and olive pressing. Actors and actresses perform for the visitors and explain the kind of life that Jews led in ancient times.

Industrial Area of Katzrin   04-696-2412

Golan Heights Winery: This winery offers a one-hour tour at the visitors center. It includes an introductory movie, a visit to the oak barrel cellar and wine tasting.

Katzrin Industrial Area   04-696-8435
www.golanwines.co.il

Museum of Golani Division Heroism: This memorial site is at the Golani Junction overlooking a pine forest. The Golani Brigade fought fierce battles in this region. The museum commemorates those who fell, and tells the story of their battles. There are both indoor and outdoor exhibits, including some tanks.

Golani Junction, between Highways 65 and 77
04-676-7215

Lake Hula Bird Observatory: Once a marshland, state leaders in the 50s and 60s decided to drain the Hula Lake in order to eradicate malaria, and provide space for living and agriculture. However the damage to the ecosystem was immense, and attempts have been made to reverse this process. Today the Hula National Park offers visitors boat, bike and walking tours around the pools that have been recreated. Large flocks nest here year-round and others rest on their route from Europe to Africa and back. You need between 1 and 3 hours here. There is a gift shop and snack bar and it is wheelchair-accessible.

Hula Valley   04-693-7069
bit.ly/tyk2hua

Zip Line at Manara

Manara: A full outdoor activity center with a cable car ride to the top of the mountain. Halfway up you can do some rappelling, rock climbing and get on a 600-foot zip line. For the more moderate guests in the group there is an alpine slide and trampoline at the bottom. At the very top there is a nice pool and magnificent views of Kiryat Shemona and all the way to Lebanon.

Kiryat Shemona-45 km north of   04-690-5830
    Tiberia, off Route 90   www.cliff.co.il

Canada Center: The Canada Center has something for everyone in the family: ice skating in the largest rink in Israel, bowling, swimming pools, water slide, spa, shooting range, a 7D cinema with moving chairs and other activities. Kosher restaurant.

Metulla   04-695-0370
1 Ha-Rishonim St.   www.canada-centre.co.il

Teva Naot Shoe Factory Outlet: This is a large store with good prices on Naot shoes.

Kibbutz Naot Mordechai,   073-212-0183
    off Route 90   www.tevanaot.co.il

ATV/tractors Havat Hayarden: Ages 16 and up with a license can drive the ATVs. Two can go together on a great path in the Golan. Loads of fun for the whole family.

Mishmar Hayarden   04-900-7000, 054-774-4700
                                 www.traktoron.co.il

Kibbutz Ayelet Hashahar Shooting Range: Adults and children can shoot at moving targets with live ammunition. There is also air gun practice for the youngest members of your group. This can be combined with archery, paintball or Tomcar rides.

Hagoshrim Kayaks: A 5 km family course that begins in the Hatzbani River and continues down the Jordan River. It lasts approximately 1 ½ hours. There is a more exciting course of 6 km that lasts almost 2 hours. You can also do four-wheel ATV tours and bicycle tours here.

077-271-7500   www.kayak.co.il

Kayak Kfar Blum, Kayak Beit Hillel: Another pleasant family kayaking/rafting course lasting about 1 ½ hours.

04-694-8755, 072-395-1180   www.kayaks.co.il

Yaar Haayalim: In the Golan on Moshav Odem is a park with all types of deer and other animals with horns and antlers. The guide will teach you the difference between the animals and show you the ones used to make shofars. There is a petting corner, playground and camping facilities. The guide is excellent but bring someone who knows Hebrew. Fruit picking is also available on this moshav.

Moshav Odem   050-522-9450
                                 www.yayalim.co.il

Golan Fruits

Golan Fruits: Watch a short film followed by an interesting tour of the factory where they clean, sort and pack the apples. Then go to the orchard and pick some apples! Apple tours are available all year. Cherry tours run from May through July. Not stroller accessible.

www.pri-beresheet.co.il

Ktofoti Fruit and Vegetable Picking: Depending on the season, they offer picking a large range of vegetables and fruit. Your visit begins with herbal tea and explanations about the seasonal fruits and vegetables. Then go off and pick your own!

    Beit Lechem Hagalilit   054-550-7480
                                          www.ktofoti.co.il

Bustan Bereshit Fruit Picking and More: Different fruits for different seasons. Cherries, blackberries, pears, nectarines, peaches, grapes, figs and apples. Pick some delicious fruit and enjoy some of the many activities such as ATVs, carting, horseback rides and rope climbing. Activities change. Not stroller accessible.

    Ein Zivan, Golan   04-699-3610
                                            www.enzivan.co.il

Self-Fruit Picking in Odem: In a small village called Odem, in the north of the Golan Heights, you can enjoy picking cherries, figs, peaches, berries and a lot more. There are shaded areas for picnics, and a shop with homemade items. Open from the beginning of June until the end of September every day from 8:30.

    Moshav Odem, Golan Heights   050-845-0962, 054-260-0130
                                          www.katifodem.co.il

Amiad Artist Colony: A quaint village off the beaten path, with several craft shops. You can find ceramics, Judaica, and all types of unusual gifts in this colony.

    Off route 808

Ski Chairlift to the Top of Mt. Hermon: This is a worthwhile ride. The scenery is beautiful and so are the views from the top. When there is snow in the winter, this is a ski resort.

    Take Route 99 east to Route 989 north to the village of Neve Ativ, Mt. Hermon.
    www.hermon.com/mt_hermon/

De Karina

De Karina Chocolate Workshop and Tour: This homemade chocolate shop offers workshops for the whole family.

Kibbutz Ein Zivon   04-699-3622

www.de-karina.co.il

Nimrod's Fortress

Nimrod's Fortress National Park: This large fortress was built during the years 1227-1230 on Mt. Hermon. A visit here can be an exciting one. It is full of dark tunnels, protruding towers, cisterns and steps! Lots of great climbing opportunities and plenty of places to hide. A bit out of the way but worthwhile if you like fortresses. Spectacular view of the Galilee and Golan Heights.

Nimrod's Fortress National Park, Route 989 off Route 99
04-694-9277   bit.ly/tyk2nimrod

Tel Faher, Mitzpe Golani: This is a memorial to the soldiers of the Golani Brigade who died here in 1967. Children can enter the Syrian bunkers and trenches and climb on the tank.

Tel Faher, off Route. 99. Turn right above Banias.

Golan Hikes

Note: When hiking in the Golan, do not stray past the paths. Pay attention to warning signs, and don't climb over any fences. There may still be some mines around.

Nahal El Al

Nahal El Al Reserve: This spring is in the El Al River in the southern part of the Golan. It contains two beautiful waterfalls which have carved through the basalt stone. The Black Waterfall gets its name from the black color of the basaltic stone. The second waterfall is the White Waterfall, which gets its name from the white chalkstone it uncovers. Each waterfall has its own pool. There are different options for this hike, ranging from short to long. The route begins in Henyon HaMapalim, near Moshav Avnei Eitan. The short route is about a 45-minute walk to the waterfall. Most of it is relatively flat and not too difficult. There are many steps, however, to access the waterfall.

Golan Heights   Moshav Avnei Eitan

Tel Dan

Tel Dan Nature Reserve: The Dan River is the largest source of the Jordan River. This is a beautiful park setting with wheelchair-accessible, shaded trails. There is a cold natural pool available for a dip, and you can see a lot of local wildlife.

25 km southeast of Metulla near Kibbutz Dan on Route 99

04-695-1579   bit.ly/tyk2teldan

Ein Tina: This is truly a family hike. During warm summer days you have a chance to enjoy the cool spring and waterfall. Walking is inside the water and the spring is swimmable. There is also a dry path next to the spring for those who want to stay dry. The walk begins in a shallow stream which will split after a short walk. Those who want to stay dry will go right and walk among the shady trees up to the hilltop. Water lovers will go left and meet with a flow in the stream. The walk is on basalt stones, so use care. After about 20 minutes you will reach the Ein Tina waterfall, where the spring breaks out through a pipe. Admire the lovely view of Hula Valley and walk back the way you came.

> From Mishmar Hayarden junction, turn north to road 918 (Gonen-Ramot). About 23 km after the Pekak Bridge there is a Hebrew sign to the spring. Follow the dirt road until you reach a wide space where you can park.

Nahal Snir (Hetzbani): This hike has beautiful scenery and rushing streams. It can be completed in an hour, depending on how much time you spend swimming. Most of the walk is in water up to your ankles, but you do have to clamber over rocks and duck under tree limbs. There are also currents in the stream that are a lot of fun and here you can actually swim. There is a lovely restaurant here as well, called Dag al Hadan. You sit by the stream and enjoy fresh fish and pasta. A real country environment and excellent food.

> Near Kibbutz Ma'ayan Baruch   bit.ly/tyk2snir

Mitzpe Hashalom (Peace Vista): This is a lovely place to stop on your way to or from the Golan. It is an overlook which allows you to see all of Lake Kinneret. From here, you can see Israel, Jordan and Syria. There are also some nice trails here on the reserve if you have the time.

> Route 98, just south of Nahal El Al

Nahal Zavitan: This is the easiest of the serious hikes. It includes waterfalls, pools and canyons, and is truly breathtaking. This is a half-day trip with a circular trail. Here you will experience very impressive hexagonal pools. At the second one you can enjoy a swim. When you are finished there, go back to the path and continue down to a waterfall and large pool. Here you can take a refreshing dip before you begin your ascent to the parking lot.

> Yehudiya Parking Area 8 kilometers southwest of Katzrin on Route 87
> bit.ly/tyk2yehudiya

Nahal Yehudiya: This is a wild and challenging hike, with sensational waterfalls and refreshing pools. You *must* be a swimmer. The hike begins in an abandoned Syrian village and then continues for a bit until you reach the first pool. Take a swim and relax; the more challenging part of the hike is still ahead of you. You will walk back and forth across the river several times until finally reaching a long ladder on which you must descend directly into the pool below. If you choose a busy day you may have to wait a while for your turn. You will then swim across to the next landing and descend again into another pool using rungs embedded in the rock. After this pool you continue on the trail. You will soon come to a junction in the trail. One route takes you for three more hours of hiking; the other trail leads back to the parking lot.

bit.ly/tyk2yehudiya

Nahal Dvora in the Jilabun Nature Reserve: This hike includes ruins, two waterfalls with pools, and lovely flowing stream s. It is a half day-hike and of medium difficulty. You must be adept at walking over rocks. It is *not* path walking. The first waterfall you come to is the Dvora Waterfall. It is 10 meters high, and gives an incredibly refreshing massage. You will then continue along the red trail to the Jilabune Waterfall. It is 40 meters high and the second highest in Israel. You can swim in the pool here and even behind the waterfall. Magnificent scenery here. When you finish your swim go back up the way you came down and follow the blue trail to the car.

www.parks.org.il

Banias Nature Reserve: This reserve contains ruins of ancient cities as well the Banias waterfall. You can spend hours walking the trails and exploring the ruins. Banias Falls Park has a large parking lot. From the entrance a trail leads down to the river (about a 45-minute walk round trip), including the suspended trail running above the river. Banias Springs Park has a smaller parking lot. Here you can visit Pan's Cave and the ruins around the cave. You cannot go into the waterfall at Banias.

Upper Golan east of Kibbutz Snir on Road 99
Springs entrance:04-690-2577   bit.ly/tyk2banias
Falls entrance: 04-695-0272

Gamla Nature Reserve

Gamla Nature Reserve: Huge vultures live here. From the main entrance a 600-yard Vulture Trail leads to the bird-watching post on the face of the cliff. Also from the entrance, a 90-minute trail leads to the Gamla waterfall—the highest in Israel, at 51 meters. There is no swimming here.

Gamla Junction-Daliyot Junction Road (No. 869). Go north for about 2 km to the turnoff sign to the reserve.

04-682-2282/3   bit.ly/tyk2gamla

Dead Sea Region

The beauty of the desert landscape in combination with the blue waters of the Dead Sea and an incredible mountain backdrop make this area one of the most breathtaking places in the world. Enjoy beaches, hiking or luxury hotels. See an oasis with natural wildlife and visit Masada. You won't be disappointed.

Qumran National Park

Qumran National Park: Qumran is famous for the magnificent legacy left to us by the Essenes: the Dead Sea Scrolls. Bedouin shepherds found seven ancient scrolls in a local cave, preserved in pottery jars. Some of these scrolls are on display at "The Shrine of the Book" in the Israel Museum. Use an audio guide to tour the paths and learn how the Essenes lived. Visit the ritual baths, kitchen, dining halls and the watch tower. See the 10-minute movie about the area on large screens, and visit the small museum. The visit takes about an hour. Great gift shop. Worth a stop.

Route 90, opposite the shore of the Dead Sea

02-994-2235   bit.ly/tyk2qumran

Ahava Visitors Center: A quick stop for the adults! Through the glass windows observe Ahava products being manufactured. Buy Ahava products at a reasonable price.

Route 90, Mitzpe Shalem (about 10 minutes past Qumran)
02-994-5117

En Gedi Nature Reserve

En Gedi Nature Reserve: A fabulous nature reserve with cliffs, streams, waterfalls and tropical reeds. This is a spectacular sight in the middle of a desert. Nahal David is the main attraction. There are clearly marked trails that take you past natural pools to the beautiful waterfall at the top. You can swim here and go into the waterfalls. There are many steps, but it is not difficult. Also look for ibex and other wildlife in the area.

Along Road 90 (Dead Sea), approx. 1 km north of Kibbutz En Gedi
08-658-4285   bit.ly/tyk2gedi

En Gedi Antiquities National Park: Adjacent to the En Gedi Nature Reserve, you will find the remains of a Byzantine-period synagogue. The remains include inscriptions on the floor, a list of generations from Adam to Japheth, a list of months and signs of the zodiac, and an oath swearing the reader to maintain the secrecy of the settlement. Many scholars believe the secret was the process of manufacturing perfume from persimmons, which brought En Gedi fame in the ancient world.

Route 90 (Dead Sea) near the En Gedi Nature Reserve
08-658-4285, 03-776-2163   bit.ly/tyk2gedi

Nahal Arugot: Can you find the deer?

Nahal Arugot: Not far from Nahal David is another beautiful reserve. It is about an hour-long hike to *The Hidden Waterfall*. There are shallow pools and it is not a difficult hike, though there are many steps.

En Gedi   08-658-4285
                                           bit.ly/tyk2gedi

Dead Sea

Dead Sea: The Dead Sea borders Israel and Jordan. It is a salt lake, with banks over 400 meters below sea level, the lowest point in the world. The salt makes floating easy and its mud is used for therapeutic and cosmetic treatments. En Gedi Beach is an option if you want to take a dip in a public, free beach. Wear water shoes as the beach is made of small stones, not sand.

Dead Sea Exploration Boat Excursions: Noam Bedein takes you on an amazing journey on the Dead Sea. Children ages four and up can participate in this educational experience. See salt formations, salt cliffs, stalactites and caves. Boats can hold up to 10 people and additional boats are available. Tours can be 90 minutes or three hours.

Mitzpe Shalem   054-559-8977

www. Dead sea revival.org

Masada: Ride the cable car, take the Ramp Path or walk up the Snake Path. However you arrive at the top you will see some of the most impressive ruins in the country. Tile floors, mikvot, and store rooms, including models of how Masada looked in the past. There are beautiful desert views, and seeing the sunrise from the top is always a treat. The visitors center includes a museum, a gift shop and a model of Masada. Stop and look. Try to visit early morning or late afternoon. It is very hot during the day.

18 km south of En Gedi on Route 90   08-658-4207/8

bit.ly/tyk2masada

Masada Sound and Light Show: The show is in Hebrew but headsets for English are available for 15 NIS. The show tells the story of the rebels' last days at the fortress. It's quite amazing against the dramatic backdrop of the western side of Masada. Call ahead to confirm availability of tickets. The show takes place from March through October on Tuesday and Thursday nights at 9:00.

Access is via the Arad-Masada road only (3199)

08-995-9333   bit.ly/tyk2masada

Flour Caves: A descent into a magnificent white limestone rock canyon with a short hike. There was a small section through a dark cave but that has closed due to erosion. This is easy even for young children, and they will be delighted with the ease with which they can lift giant rocks. You will come out covered in white dust, hence the name *flour caves*. The scenery is beautiful just before sundown. This canyon is difficult to find if no one in your party has been there before, but it is worth the effort.

On the Arava-Dead Sea Road, turn onto an unpaved road between kilometers 193 and 194. Look for signs to Nachal Perazim or The Flour Cave. The road ends at a car park and it is about a 15-minute walk through canyons to reach the cave.

Beersheva

Beersheva is one of the oldest cities in Israel. Abraham built wells here, Isaac built an altar here and King Saul made a fort here. Tel Beersheva is just outside the city and is thought to be the well Abraham dug and made an oath over with seven ewes with the king of Gerar.

Air Force Museum

Israel Air Force Museum: This museum contains more than 100 planes that played a role in Israel's history. It includes the Boeing 707 that was used in the famous rescue of an Air France plane in 1976, that had been hijacked to Entebbe, Uganda. There is a brief film inside the plane about the rescue. There is also an exhibit in memory of Ilan Ramon, the hero killed in the Columbia shuttle disaster. This museum offers indoor and outdoor exhibits, and planes that children can climb into.

Route 2357, 7 km west of Beersheva   08-990-6888

www.ilmuseums.com.iaf.org.il

Abraham's Well Visitors' Center: This visitors' center requires that you take a one-hour tour in order to finally see the well that Abraham dug. There is a nice walkway lit with stars , and a 3D movie about Abraham. The remainder of the tour is explanations that are a bit basic and tedious. With the exception of the movie, children may find this tour too long and not engaging. You must call to schedule an English tour.

2 Derech Hevron   08-623-4613

www.beer-sheva.muni.il

Lunada Children's Museum

Lunada Children's Museum: Lunada is a world-class children's museum and a completely "please touch me" museum. It contains many diverse activities and games which encourage general knowledge, exploration, investigation, reasoning, basic skills and much more. Recommended for ages 2–12, but older children can also enjoy it.

25 David HaRe'uveni Street   08-622-6926

www.lunada.co.il

Children's Park

Children's Park: Immediately outside Lunada is an amazing children's playground. It includes two zip lines, very long tube slides, climbing facilities, a ropes course, unique swings and more. The area is covered, and therefore practical even in the heat of the day. There is no charge to use this park.

Old Turkish Railway Station (The Train Yard): For train enthusiasts, this a short stop in the area. There is a mini museum with a few interactive games on the premises. There are four old trains, including a lounge car, which you can enter. The grounds are nice for a picnic, but hot in the summer. You can call ahead for a guided tour.

65 Tuviyahu Blvd.   08-623-4613

www.katar70414.org.il

Carasso Science Park:

Carasso Science Park: Another world-class museum. This indoor/outdoor science park allows visitors to experience the scientific research process through displays, activities, games and explanations. It covers many topics such as light, communication, genetic code and nuclear energy. Much of it is underground and cool, even in the summer. Good for all ages but geared to school-age children and older.

79 HaAtsmaut Street   08-625-2600

www.sci-park.co.il

Negev and Eilat

Tel Arad National Park: Tel Arad encompasses the remains of a Canaanite city from the Bronze Age and fortresses built by the kings of Judah. There is an overnight campground. If arranged in advance, there is a possibility of pottery painting for children or a lantern tour in the evening, if you are staying nearby. Do not go in the heat of the day and always take water. You can drive right up to the fortress.

    Route 80, Near Arad   08-699-2447
                                             bit.ly/tyk2arad

Sde Boker

Kibbutz Sde Boker: This kibbutz was established in 1952 and attracted the public's attention when David Ben Gurion moved there with his wife Paula. The hut in which he lived until his death in 1973 is preserved as it was when he lived there. It contains archives, and adjacent to his hut is a small museum dedicated to Ben Gurion and his love for the Negev. He and his wife are both buried here at a beautiful lookout point. Ibexes and gazelles wander freely here.

    Route 25   08-659-2100
                                            www.bgh.org.il

En Avdat: This is a family hike through a landscaped canyon, with springs and lots of wildlife. There are two ladders to climb, but it is not a difficult hike. If you have two cars, it is best to park one of them at the end of the hike, otherwise you will have to walk back. It is not a circular hike.

Sde Boker   08-655-5684

En Avdat National Park   bit.ly/tyk2avdat

En Avdat National Park

En Avdat National Park: From the third century BCE to the third century CE, Avdat was station number 62 on the incense route, and a small Nabatean settlement. Avdat is officially a World Heritage site. Get to know the Nabateans with a film at the information shop. You can then drive to the site. You will see remains from the early and late Roman periods and the Byzantine period. You'll see a bathhouse, store caves, churches, Roman towers, and more. A huge earthquake in the seventh century destroyed Avdat and it was abandoned.

Negev Desert   08-655-1511

Avdat National Park   www.parks.il

Mamshit National Park

Mamshit National Park: A World Heritage Site, Mamshit is an ancient Nabatean desert city located on what was once the Incense Route. It is a unique testimony to a culture that has disappeared and underscores the significance of incense and spices transported from the Far East. You can see the remains of inns for commercial caravans, a dwelling from a wealthy family, as well as other Nabatean dwellings and horse stables. There is a fascinating street with a row of rooms on either side, which served as shops.

On holidays this turns into a colorful and lively market.

7 km east of Dimona, on the main road to Eilat

bit.ly/tyk2mamshit

Museum of Bedouin Culture: This museum focuses on the Bedouin people who have long lived in the Negev. On display is carpet weaving, wool spinning and bread baking, plus an archeological section complete with a display of caves from the Mishnaic and Talmudic eras. Kids will love climbing through them. Donkey rides are also available.

Route 325 off Route 31   08-991-3394

www.joealon.org.il

Camel tour

Cameland, Negev Camel Ranch: Near the ancient ruins of Mamshit lies the Negev Camel Ranch. The ranch raises riding camels and it offers camel tours as well as desert hospitality and lodging. No prior experience is needed to ride. Children under 12 need to ride with an adult. Tours range from one hour to a few days.

Eastern Negev, off Route 25, near Mamshit National Park
From the entry road to Mamshit, turn left to the camel ranch.
08-655-2829   www.cameland.co.il

The Ramon Crater Visitor Center: This visitor center enables visitors to combine information about the largest *makhtesh* (erosion crater) in the world and the story of Colonel Ilan Ramon, the Israeli astronaut. This is a multimedia presentation, which is interesting for children and adults alike. I highly recommend this as your first stop at the crater!

Mitzpe Ramon   08-658-8691
Rehov Maale Ben Tur   www.parks.org.il

Ramon Crater Park (Makhtesh Ramon): This is an ideal place to study geology. This is the world's largest erosion crater. This area was once part of an ancient sea; the crater is the results of millions of years of sedimentation and erosion, as well as movement of the Great Rift Valley. You can see many layers of rock and evidence of volcanic activity, including hexagonal formations along the crater walls. Many species of animals make their homes here. The Negev highlands are home to leopards, hyenas, gazelles, wolves, red foxes, rodents and reptiles. You can visit this site for an hour or a day at any time of year. The view of the makhtesh is particularly worth seeing at sunset. If you like the Grand Canyon, you will enjoy the makhtesh.

07-658-8691/8   bit.ly/tyk2ramon

Colorful Natural Sand: This activity is free of charge and no guide is necessary. Drive into the crater via Highway 40 in the direction of Eilat. Approximately 500 meters after HaMinsara you will see a parking lot on your right. Leave your car there and look for a short staircase down. The area is filled with beautiful colors of natural sand. Bring bottles and fill them!

Astronomy Israel—Stargazing: Enjoy an evening out in the desert, near the makhtesh, learning about the wonders of the night sky. Using your eyes and telescopes observe the moon rising, constellations, planets—and if you're lucky, some meteors flashing through the sky.

052-544-9789   www.astronomyisrael.com

Alpaca Farm

Alpaca Farm: Over 400 alpacas and llamas make their home at this farm. You can see the process of wool making here, from shearing to spinning. Wool products are available for purchase. Children under about 60 pounds can ride an alpaca; everyone else can ride a camel. You can hand-feed these animals as well.

From Beersheva, Route 40 south toward Mitzpe Ramon. Turn off the main road at the gas station.

08-658-8047, 052-897-7010   www.alpaca.co.il

Jeep Tours, Rappelling

Jeep Tours & Other Activities in the Makhtesh: With Deep Desert Israel (one of several tour companies), you can travel through the makhtesh in an air-conditioned Jeep, stopping to learn about the history and sights you can't see from the road. Amazing! Also available: rappelling, stargazing, helicopter tours, Bedouin hospitality and hiking.

052-220-1776   www.deepdesertisrael.com

Timna Park

Timna Park: Right in the middle of the Red Sea Desert, this park has in-credible scenery, history and action fun. The entrance to this park has a multimedia presentation on a revolving stage. The presentation discusses the origin of the copper serpent, the ancient Egyptian gods and the an-tiquities in Timna. You can see a natural stone arch, ancient mines, rock drawings and inscriptions. There are amazing natural rock formations of red sandstone, Solomon's Pillars and Timna Lake. There is a family activity center. Children can sail in pedal boats, fill bottles with colored sand or cast a copper coin from King Solomon's time. Camel rides are also available.

25 km north of Eilat   08-631-6756

www.parktimna.co.il

Red Canyon

Red Canyon: This is a beautiful canyon hike right outside of Eilat. The sandstone walls are predominantly red, with other shades of pink and purple. It involves some climbing and walking on some narrow ledges, but the scenery is magnificent, and the hike is under two hours roundtrip. It is magnificent around sunset, but you would want to be almost back to the starting point by then.

North of Eilat on Highway 12   East side of the road

Hai Bar Yotvata Nature Reserve: This reserve breeds and nurtures endangered animals and Biblical wildlife that have disappeared from Israel, with the goal of releasing them back into the wild. You can tour the area in your own car with a guide from the reserve. Watch for Asian and African wild ass, Arabian oryx, gazelles, addax (white antelope) and ostrich.

Half hour north of Eilat   08-637-3057
Route 90   bit.ly/tyk2yotvata

Tubing in Eilat

Eilat Beaches: The North Beach and South Beach are public beaches. You will find all types of water action on the North Beach. You can go paragliding, banana boating, tubing or rent paddle boats. South Beach has the Coral Reserve, Dolphin Reef and the Underwater Observatory.

The Underwater Observatory

The Underwater Observatory: This is a unique aquarium and marine museum. Underwater observation decks let you watch the sealife in its natural habitat. In the aquarium, you can see a coral reef tank, shark pool, turtle pool, stingray pool and more. Kids will appreciate the Oceanarium, a simulator motion theater, where spectators sit in moving seats and watch an audiovisual show offering the true sensation of an amazing journey under the sea.

Marine Park, Eilat   08-636-4200
                                          www.coralworld.co.il

Dolphin Reef: Swim, snorkel or dive with dolphins. Children must be eight and older for the dives. See dolphins in their natural habitat. You can purchase videos and pictures of your dive at the end of your stay. Make reservations in advance.

Southern Beach, Eilat 08-630-0100
www.dolphinreef.co.il

Coral Reserve: This is a great place to see the fish and coral. You can rent snorkeling equipment here. Be sure to wear water shoes that stay on your feet! Lockers and showers are available.

Taba Road, Coral Beach 08-637-6829
bit.ly/tyk2coral

Ice Mall

Ice Mall: Here you can combine ice skating with shopping. The ice rink is breathtaking and spans about 6,000 square feet. Professional skaters sometimes perform here. There are wooden stands for observers. At times it is crowded and noisy. For ages 6 and up. Bring your own socks to wear with skates! There are many more kid-friendly activities at the mall, including laser tag, a roller coaster, and a virtual reality experience for the older adventurer.

Yam Suf Tower Spiral House 08-637-9552
8 Kampen St. www.icemalleilat.co.il

Ice Age: Experience the world of ice. You can ride an ice slide, visit an igloo, and see ice sculptures. Adults can get a drink at the ice bar. Warm clothes are provided at the entrance. A nice place to cool off, but it's expensive and the melting ice can make things slippery. You can see this in under 1 hour. Ages 3 and up.

    08-633-2225   www.ice-space.co.il

Parasailing in Eilat

Red Sea Parasailing: Parasailing and other water sports.

    Derech Hayam   08-637-8504, 052-271-2178

                                    www.rsp-eilat.co.il

Aqua Sport: Diving excursions, includes introductory dives. Paragliding.
Coral Beach   08-633-4404
                                     www.aqua-sport.co.il

Conversions

Women's Shoes Men's Shoes

US	EUR	US	EUR
5	36	7	39½
6	37	8	41
7	38	9	42
8	39	10	43
9	40	11	44½
		12	46

Temperature

Degrees Fahrenheit	Degrees Celsius
32	0
60	15.5
70	21.1
80	26.6
90	32.2
98.6	37
100	37.7

Distance

To change kilometers to miles, multiply kilometers by 0.621.

Kilometers	Miles
1	0.62
2	1.2
3	1.9
4	2.5
5	3.1
8	5.0

Great One-Day Itineraries

When our family travels, we start out by 8:00 A.M. and return after dark. We take pita, hummus and pickles along for lunch, so we are really on the road for a full day. If you are more likely to start out late and end early, you may want to cut one or two things off the itinerary! Remember to make reservations and most of all—plan ahead!

Jerusalem

A. Start with a visit to the Kotel and an early tour of the Kotel tunnels. Then move on to a tour of the City of David, including Hezkiahu's water tunnel. Bring flashlights and prepare to be wet. Take a break, change into dry clothes and take a ride on the Time Elevator near Ben Yehuda pedestrian mall. Spend the early evening shopping and relaxing at the outdoor cafés on Ben Yehuda.

B. Ein Yael, the Biblical Zoo and/or the Aquarium are a good combination.

C. Visit the Bloomfield Science Museum or the Israel Museum (aim for the children's wing). Then burn off some energy at Ammunition Hill before taking a guided tour at the Begin Museum.

D. Spend the morning at Yad Vashem visiting the many different pavilions, including the children's memorial. The Herzl museum and Har Herzl is a great follow-up after Yad Vashem.

Around Jerusalem

A. Start the morning with Dig for a Day (really only half a day). Proceed to Speedi Kef for an Alpine slide. Spend an hour or two at Latrun, and at closing time head for Mini Israel.

Kfar Etzion

B. Begin your day at a wood or bread-baking workshop. Visit the sound and light show at Kfar Etzion and learn the history of the area. Buy some Naot at the factory outlet, and finish your day with a tour of the Biyar Aqueduct in Efrat. If you prefer extreme sports, or a visit to a petting zoo, visit Deerland, opposite the entry to Kfar Etzion.

C. Take a tour of the Zomet Institute and complete your day with a bread workshop or woodworking workshop.

Dead Sea Area

A. Start out in Genesis Land in the morning; allow about 3 hours. Spend the afternoon in the Tekhelet factory. Complete the day with tractor riding in the desert.

B. You can easily combine Masada, the Dead Sea and En Gedi, including the Ein Gedi synagogue ruins. The cable car times vary with the holidays and seasons, so always check the times. If you still have energy, the flour caves are a great visit just before sunset in the non-rainy season. If you have hiked En Gedi, consider Nahal Arugot.

Beit Shean Area

Beit Shean National Park is a good starting point, as it gets very hot later in the day. Visit the Crusader castle of Belvoir and from there spend time in Sachne where you can swim and have lunch. The Kangaroo farm is right next door—no need to move the car, and it is open into the early evening hours in the summer. Consider making this trip when Beit Shean National Park is offering its night program, and make the National Park your last stop instead of your first. You need reservations for this program.

Lower Galil

A. Start out at Megiddo National Park, see the sacrificial altar and walk through the water tunnel (it no longer contains water), and go on to Beit Shearim National park to walk through the catacombs. Drive to Zippori; try to arrange a mosaic-making session in advance. End at Yodfat, a great monkey farm with a host of other animals, many of which walk around freely.

B. Hamat Gader is good for a full or half day. You may want to combine it with Tiberias or activities around Lake Kinneret.

C. Climb the Arbel (not for people who are afraid of heights or edges) and view the entire Galil from the top. There are caves to stop and look in on the way to the top. If you do not have a second car at the top, descend carefully. Then visit Kefar Tavor and either go to the Marzipan Museum for some creative food sculpting or Dvorat Hatavor for a bee/honey experience.

Negev Area

Drive to Sde Boker, visit the memorial site of Ben Gurion and his wife Paula. Then hike the canyon of En Avdat, with its ladders and stone steps.

Drive toward Mitzpe Ramon, and make your first stop the visitors center. Then take an air-conditioned Jeep ride in the makhtesh. Break for dinner and attend a stargazing session after nightfall.

Start with a visit to the Air Force Museum, then choose either the Lunada (children 2–12) or the Carasso Science Park (for older children).

Mediterranean Coast (4 one-day trips)

A. Combine some sightseeing and adventure. Start with a morning trip to Zichron Yaakov. Visit the Aaronson house and take an English tour, try to get a workshop at Tut-Neyar, and have lunch on the cobblestone street. Finish off with a visit to Park Alona with a walk through the water tunnels.

B. Return to Zichron Yaakov for a tour of the Carmel or Tishbi winery. Spend an hour at the beautiful gardens of Ramat Hanadiv. Drive south to Caesaria. Visit the ruins and visitor center and then take a speedboat ride, or a slow boat at Kibbutz S'dot Yam (Kef Yam), by Caesaria. People not interested in the speedboat can rest on the beach and watch the others.

C. Start with a climb up to the Carmel Caves and see the movie inside the cave. Visit the galleries of Ein Hod and arrange for a pottery-making session. Complete your day at Atlit for a bit of more recent history.

D. Rosh Hanikra is a good starting point. The cable car ride is pleasant, as is the scenery. You can combine this with Akko, Haifa, Atlit or a trip to one of the many coastal beaches. If you choose Haifa, I recommend a short hike on the Hanging Bridge of Nesher Park.

Netanya

A. Visit the parrot farm in the morning in Kfar Hess. Hold the parrots, feed the animals and visit the petting zoo. Spend the afternoon on the Netanya beach. Don't forget to take the elevator up and down. Go for a sunset horseback riding trip on the beach. In the evening, walk the square and see the vendors displaying their crafts. Older children may want to try go-karting at Karting Poleg.

B. Take a tour of the Roladin Bakery right near Netanya, bake some cookies and have lunch in their restaurant. Try some go-karting in the afternoon or take a ride to Beit Oren and ride the Tomcars. This requires traveling a distance of about a half hour out of Netanya.

Around Tel Aviv

A. South of Tel Aviv: Rehovot. Start with the Ayalon Institute tour, visit the Weizman Science Park, and finish with a Tnuva factory tour.

B. East of Tel Aviv: Start out at Neot Kedumim, take a tour, take the tram and see the Sukkot. Allow a few hours. Spend the afternoon at the Ben Shemen monkey park, Afrikef. Return to Old Yaffo and walk the port or take a boat ride at sunset.

Tel Aviv

A. Begin with a tour of the Palmach Museum, maybe visit Museum Haaretz next door as well. Take a Coca Cola factory tour, spend some time and eat at the Azrieli Center. Then proceed to the observatory at the top for a beautiful view of the city.

B. Spend half a day at the Tel Aviv Safari, then visit Park Hayarkon. Bike, boat or play mini golf. Early evening is a good time for Luna Park.

C. Spend the morning at the Steinhardt Museum of Natural History and the afternoon at Beit Hatfutzot.

Golan

A. Start out by exploring Nimrod's Fortress and its many hidden tunnels. Move on to Mt. Hermon and take the ski lift to the top. Stop off at Mitzpe Golani, climb into the trenches and sit on the tank. Finish the day with a trip to the Naot factory, and rafting down the Jordan River.

B. Begin your day with the Manara activity center. Decide on a time limit as kids can spend the whole day here. Take a refreshing walk through Tel

Dan and dip in the cold pool there.

C. Take a real hike in the Golan. Nahal Yehudia, Nahal Zavitan or Nahal Jilabun are all challenging hikes and more suited to older children and teens. Arrive early and plan to spend a good part of the day here.

Eilat

A. Spend the morning at at the Underwater Observatory. Spend the afternoon at Dolphin Reef, swimming with the dolphins. You can do some parasailing, tubing or banana boating in the late afternoon. Walk the promenade in the evening for some shopping and amusement park rides.

B. Start out snorkeling in the morning at Coral Beach. Spend the afternoon ice skating at the Ice Mall or experience the world of ice at Ice Age. Hike the Red Canyon in the late afternoon—but plan to finish before sunset.

C. Spend the day at Timna Park—drive, hike, swim and do some creative activities.

Index

About the Author

Aileen lives in Plainview, New York with her husband, Ben. She teaches 2nd grade at the Hebrew Academy of Nassau County in Plainview. She spends most of her vacation time in Israel with her family and friends.